PENPALS for Handwriting

Year 4 Teacher's Book

Gill Budgell   Kate Ruttle

Supported by the

National Handwriting Association
Promoting good practice

Contents

● denotes the introduction of new content

Scope and sequence

Units introducing new letters or joins are flagged with coloured dots.

Foundation 1 / 3–5 years

Developing gross motor skills
1 Whole-body responses to the language of movement
2 Large movements with equipment
3 Large movements with malleable materials
4 Body responses to music

Developing fine motor skills
5 Hand and finger play
6 Making and modelling
7 Messy play
8 Links to art
9 Using one-handed tools and equipment
10 Hand responses to music

Developing patterns
11 Pattern-making
12 Investigating dots
13 Investigating straight lines and crosses
14 Investigating circles
15 Investigating curves, loops and waves
16 Investigating joined straight lines and angled patterns
17 Investigating eights and spirals

Foundation 2 / Primary 1

Term 1
1 Dots
2 Straight lines and crosses
3 Circles
4 Waves
5 Loops and bridges
6 Joined straight lines
7 Angled patterns
8 Eights
9 Spirals
10 Left-to-right orientation
11 Mix of patterns
12 Review of patterns

Term 2
13 Introducing long-legged giraffe letters: *l*
14 Practising long-legged giraffe letters: *l, i*
15 Practising long-legged giraffe letters: *u, t*
16 Practising long-legged giraffe letters: *j, y*
17 Practising all the long-legged giraffe letters: *l, i, t, u, j, y*
18 Introducing one-armed robot letters: *r*
19 Practising one-armed robot letters: *b, n*
20 Practising one-armed robot letters: *h, m*
21 Practising one-armed robot letters: *k, p*
22 Practising all the one-armed robot letters: *r, b, n, h, m, k, p*
23 Practising all the long-legged giraffe and one-armed robot letters
24 Reviewing all the long-legged giraffe and one-armed robot letters

Term 3
25 Introducing curly caterpillar letters: *c*
26 Practising curly caterpillar letters: *a, d*
27 Practising curly caterpillar letters: *o, s*
28 Practising curly caterpillar letters: *g, q*
29 Practising curly caterpillar letters: *e, f*
30 Practising all the curly caterpillar letters: *c, a, d, o, s, g, q, e, f*
31 Practising all the curly caterpillar, long-legged giraffe and one-armed robot letters
32 Introducing zig-zag monster letters: *z*
33 Practising zig-zag monster letters: *v, w, x*
34 Practising all the zig-zag monster letters: *z, v, w, x*
35 Practising all the curly caterpillar and zig-zag monster letters
36 Reviewing all the curly caterpillar and zig-zag monster letters

Year 1 / Primary 2

Term 1
1 Practising long-legged giraffe letters
2 Writing words with *ll*
3 Introducing capitals for long-legged giraffe letters
4 Practising one-armed robot letters
5 Practising long-legged giraffe letters and one-armed robot letters
6 Introducing capitals for one-armed robot letters
7 Practising curly caterpillar letters
8 Writing words with double *ff*
9 Writing words with double *ss*
10 Introducing capitals for curly caterpillar letters

Term 2
11 Practising long-legged giraffe letters, one-armed robot letters and curly caterpillar letters
12 Practising zig-zag monster letters
13 Writing words with double *zz*
14 Mixing all the letter families
15 Practising all the capital letters
16 Practising all the numbers 0–9
17 Writing words with *ck* and *qu*
18 Practising long vowel phonemes: *ai, igh, oo*
19 Practising vowels with adjacent consonants: *ee, oa, oo*
20 End-of-term check

Term 3
21 Numbers 10–20: spacing
22 Practising *ch* unjoined
23 Introducing diagonal join to ascender: *ch*
24 Practising *ai* unjoined
25 Introducing diagonal join, no ascender: *ai*
26 Practising *wh* unjoined
27 Introducing horizontal join to ascender: *wh*
28 Practising *ow* unjoined
29 Introducing horizontal join, no ascender: *ow*
30 Assessment

Year 2 / Primary 3

Term 1
1 Practising diagonal join to ascender: *th, ch*
2 Practising diagonal join, no ascender: *ai, ay*
3 Practising diagonal join, no ascender: *ir, er*
4 Practising horizontal join to ascender: *wh, oh*
5 Practising horizontal join, no ascender: *ow, ou*
6 Introducing diagonal join to e: *ie, ue*
7 Introducing horizontal join to e: *oe, ve*
8 Introducing *ee*
9 Practising diagonal join, no ascender: *le*
10 Writing numbers 1–100

Term 2
11 Introducing diagonal join to anticlockwise letters: *ea*
12 Practising diagonal join to anticlockwise letters: *igh*
13 Practising diagonal join to anticlockwise letters: *dg, ng*
14 Introducing horizontal join to anticlockwise letters: *oo, oa*
15 Practising horizontal join to anticlockwise letters: *wra, wo*
16 Introducing mixed joins for three letters: *air, ear*
17 Practising mixed joins for three letters: *oor, our*
18 Practising mixed joins for three letters: *ing*
19 Size and spacing
20 End-of-term check

Term 3
21 Building on diagonal join to ascender: *ck, al, el, at,*
22 Building on diagonal join, no ascender: *ui, ey, aw,*
23 Building on horizontal join to ascender: *ok, ot, ob,*
24 Building on horizontal join, no ascender: *oi, ay, om*
25 Building on diagonal join to anticlockwise letters *ic, ad, ug, dd, ag*
26 Building on horizontal join to anticlockwise lette *va, vo*
27 Introducing joins to s: *as, es, is, os, ws, ns, ds, ls,*
28 Practising joining *ed* and *ing*
29 Assessment
30 Capitals

Year 3 / Primary 4

Term 1
1. Practising joining through a word in stages: no ascenders or descenders
2. Practising joining through a word in stages: parallel ascenders
3. Introducing joining from s to ascender: *sh, sl, st, sk*
4. Introducing joining from s, no ascender: *sw, si, se, sm, sn, sp, su*
5. Introducing joining from s to an anticlockwise letter: *sa, sc, sd, sg, so, sq*
6. Introducing joining from r to an ascender: *rb, rh, rk, rl, rt*
7. Introducing joining from r, no ascender: *ri, ru, rn, rp*
8. Introducing joining from r to an anticlockwise letter: *ra, rd, rg, ro*
9. Introducing joining from r to e: *are, ere, ure, ore, ire*
10. Introducing break letters: *g, j, y, f, b, p, x, z*

Term 2
11. Introducing joining to f: *if, ef, af, of*
12. Introducing joining from f to an ascender: *fl, ft*
13. Introducing joining from f, no ascender: *fe, fi, fu, fr, fy*
14. Introducing joining from f to an anticlockwise letter: *fo, fa*
15. Introducing *ff*
16. Introducing *rr*
17. Introducing *ss*
18. Introducing *qu*
19. Revising parallel ascenders and descenders
20. End-of-term check

Term 3
21. Revising joins: letter spacing
22. Revising joins: spacing between words
23. Revising joins: consistency of size
24. Revising joins: fluency
25. Revising joins: parallel ascenders
26. Revising joins: parallel ascenders and descenders
27. Revising horizontal join from r to an anticlockwise letter: *rs*
28. Revising break letters
29. Assessment
30. Revising capital letters

Year 4 / Primary 5

Term 1
1. Introducing diagonal join from p and b to ascender: *ph, pl, bl*
2. Introducing diagonal join from p and b, no ascender: *bu, bi, be, pu, pi, pe*
3. Introducing diagonal join from p and b to an anticlockwise letter: *pa, po, ps, ba, bo, bs*
4. Revising parallel ascenders and descenders: *bb, pp*
5. Break letters: *x, z*
6. Spacing in common exception words
7. Consistent size of letters
8. Relative size of capitals
9. Speed and fluency
10. End-of-term check

Term 2
11. Revising parallel ascenders
12. Revising parallel ascenders and break letters
13. Relative sizes of letters
14. Proportion of letters
15. Spacing between letters
16. Spacing between words
17. Writing at speed
18. Improving fluency
19. Speed and fluency
20. End-of-term check

Term 3
21. Consistency of size
22. Proportion
23. Spacing between letters and words
24. Size, proportion and fluency
25. Fluency: writing longer words
26. Speed and fluency
27. Revising break letters
28. Print alphabet: presentation
29. Assessment
30. Capital letters: presentation

Year 5 / Primary 6

Term 1
1. Introducing sloped writing in letter families
2. Practising sloped writing: diagonal join to ascender: *th, sh, nb, nd, ht, st*
3. Practising sloped writing: diagonal join, no ascender: *ai, ay, bu, er, ie, en*
4. Practising sloped writing: diagonal join to an anticlockwise letter: *ac, sc, bo, da, ea, ho*
5. Practising sloped writing: horizontal join to ascender: *wh, wd, oh, ol, of, ob*
6. Practising sloped writing: horizontal join, no ascender: *oi, oy, ou, op, ve*
7. Practising sloped writing: horizontal join to an anticlockwise letter: *oo, oa, wa, wo, va, vo*
8. Practising sloped writing: joining from r: *ra, re, n, ro, ru*
9. Practising sloped writing: joining from s: *sh, sa, sc, sl, sw, sp*
10. End-of-term check

Term 2
11. Practising sloped writing: proportion – joining from f to ascender: *ff, ft*
12. Practising sloped writing: size – joining from f, no ascender: *fa, fe, fi, fo, fu*
13. Different styles for different purposes: writing a paragraph
14. Practising sloped writing: speed: *ff*
15. Practising sloped writing: speed and legibility: *rr*
16. Practising sloped writing: size, proportion and spacing: *ss*
17. Practising sloped writing: building speed: *qu*
18. Different styles for different purposes: decorative alphabets
19. Different styles for different purposes
20. End-of-term check

Term 3
21. Sloped writing: proportion, joining p and b to ascenders: *ph, pl, bl*
22. Handwriting for different purposes: joining from p and b, no ascender: *bu, bu, pe, pu, pr*
23. Practising sloped writing: parallel downstrokes: *pp, bb*
24. Practising sloped writing: all double letters
25. Practising sloped writing for speed: *tual, cial*
26. Practising sloped writing for fluency
27. Personal style
28. Handwriting for different purposes: print alphabet
29. Assessment
30. Capitals

Year 6 / Primary 7

Term 1
1. Style for speed: crossbar join from t: *th, ti, tr, ta, tt*
2. Style for speed: looping from g: *gl, gi, gr, ga, gg*
3. Style for speed: looping from j and y: *je, jo, ye, yr, yo*
4. Style for speed: looping from f
5. Style for speed: different joins to s
6. Style for speed: looping from b
7. Style for speed: joining from v, w, x and z
8. Handwriting for different purposes: abbreviations
9. Spacing between words
10. End-of-term check

Term 2
11. Improving handwriting: the importance of consistent sizing
12. Improving handwriting: the importance of proportion
13. Improving handwriting: the importance of spacing
14. Improving handwriting: the importance of consistent sizing of parallel ascenders and descenders
15. Improving handwriting: the importance of closed and open letters
16. Improving handwriting: pen breaks in longer words
17. Handwriting for different purposes: annotations
18. Handwriting for different purposes
19. Choice of handwriting tools
20. End-of-term check

Term 3
21. Handwriting for different purposes: fast-joined and print letters
22. Handwriting for different purposes: note making
23. Handwriting for different purposes: neat writing
24. Handwriting for different purposes: print letters for personal details
25. Different styles of writing
26. Handwriting for different purposes: presentation
27. Handwriting for different purposes: decorated capitals
28. Handwriting for different purposes: layout
29. Assessment
30. Handwriting for different purposes: handwriting patterns

GPS scope and sequence

The *Penpals* Workbooks from Year 1 to Year 6 have a different GPS (Grammar, Punctuation and Spelling) focus in each unit. The focus type is indicated at the top of each unit page.

Year 3/Primary 4

Term 1

Unit	GPS focus
1	(S) Adding -er
2	(S) Using -ful, and -fully
3	(G) Noun phrases
4	(S) Prefixes super-, sub-
5	(G) Conjunctions: so, soon, because, sometimes
6	(G) Using adjectives
7	(S) Word families
8	(P) Capital letters and full stops
9	(S) Prefixes pre- and re-
10	(G) Determiners a, an

Term 2

Unit	GPS focus
11	(G) Prepositions
12	(S) Alphabetical order
13	(G) Using adverbs
14	(P) Apostrophes
15	(S) Suffixes
16	(S) Doubling before -ing
17	(S) Suffix -ness
18	(G) Adding suffixes to change word class -ly, -ify and -ing
19	(S) Suffix -ly
20	(S) End-of-term check

Term 3

Unit	GPS focus
21	(P) Apostrophes, contractions
22	(P)(S) it's, its
23	(S) Homophones
24	(S)(G) Homophones and punctuation
25	(S) Different uses of ch
26	(S) Suffixes -ly, -ally
27	(S) Anagrams
28	(S) Alphabetical order
29	Assessment
30	(S) Capitals

Year 4/Primary 5

Term 1

Unit	GPS focus
1	(G) Noun phrases
2	(S) Prefixes bio-, bi-
3	(S) Adverbials
4	(S) Suffixes -ing, -ed, -er
5	(S) Prefix ex-
6	(P) Inverted commas ("speech marks")
7	(S) Prefixes in-, im-, il-, ir-
8	(P) Possessive apostrophes
9	(G) Personal and possessive pronouns
10	End-of-term check

Term 2

Unit	GPS focus
11	(S) Common exception words
12	(S) Suffix -tion
13	(S) Homophones
14	(S) -ture endings
15	(G)(S) Noun phrases, -ssion endings
16	(S) Using homophones ai, ey, ay, eigh
17	(P) Inverted commas ("speech marks")
18	(G) Standard English was/were
19	(G) Possessive pronouns
20	End-of-term check

Term 3

Unit	GPS focus
21	(S) Pronouncing ou
22	(S) Pronouncing y
23	(S) Noun phrases
24	(G) Fronted adverbials
25	(G) Standard English have done/has done
26	(S) Prefixes dis-, mis-
27	(G) Pronouns
28	Presentation: Print alphabet
29	Assessment
30	Presentation: Capital letters

Penpals for Handwriting: rationale

Even in this technological, computer-literate age, good handwriting remains fundamental to our children's educational achievement. *Penpals for Handwriting* is the only handwriting programme to offer a progression from 3–11 years and will help you teach children to develop fast, fluent and legible handwriting. If you would like advice on implementing a handwriting policy at your school, you can find this on our website: education.cambridge.org/PenpalsWelcome.

Traditional principles in the contemporary classroom

We believe that:

1. A flexible, fluent and legible handwriting style empowers children to write with confidence and creativity. This is an entitlement that needs careful progression and skilful discrete teaching that is frequent and continues beyond the initial foundation stages.

2. Handwriting is a developmental process with its own distinctive stages of sequential growth. We have identified five stages that form the basic organisational structure of *Penpals*:

   (i) Physical preparation for handwriting: gross and fine motor skills leading to mark-making, patterns and letter formation (Foundation, 3–5 years)

   (ii) Securing correct letter formation (Key Stage 1, 5–6 years)

   (iii) Beginning to join along with a focus on relative size and spacing (Key Stage 1, 6–7 years)

   (iv) Securing the joins along with a focus on break letters, legibility, consistency and quality (Lower Key Stage 2, 7–9 years)

   (v) Practising speed, fluency and developing a personalised style for different purposes (Upper Key Stage 2, 9–11 years)

3. Handwriting must also be practised discretely and in context. Beyond the initial foundation stages, *Penpals* provides Workbooks for handwriting practice in the context of age-appropriate spelling, punctuation and grammar. Learning to associate the kinaesthetic handwriting movement with the visual letter pattern and the aural phonemes will help children with learning to spell. However, *Penpals* always takes a 'handwriting first' approach.

4. Choosing the writing implement best suited to the task is an important part of a handwriting education. A *Penpals* Font CD-ROM supports practitioners who wish to use the *Penpals* font consistently in all aspects of teaching and learning.

A practical approach

Penpals offers a practical, active learning, approach to support the delivery of handwriting teaching in response to the increased demands of the National Curriculum 2014.

- **Time:** *Penpals'* focus on whole-class teaching from an interactive whiteboard, with key teaching points clearly identified, allows effective teaching in the time available.
- **Planning:** *Penpals* helps with long-, medium- and short-term planning for each year group, correlated to national guidelines.
- **Practice:** *Penpals* offers pupil Practice Books, as well as Workbooks, with their own internal structure of excellent models for finger tracing, tracing, copying and independent writing.
- **Assessment:** *Penpals* offers many opportunities for assessment, including: self-assessment questions and challenges throughout the Practice Books and Workbooks; two or three assessment units in each year group and assessment ideas in the Teacher's Books. The *Penpals for Handwriting Intervention Programme* also provides further information, activities and checklists.
- **Motivation:** *Penpals* is attractive and well-designed with clear links between all of the elements in each year group. The materials are written with the support of children, classroom assistants, teachers, and handwriting experts to stimulate and motivate children.
- **ICT:** Use the *Penpals* Interactives to enrich and extend the children's handwriting experiences.

A few words from the experts ...

Handwriting is the bedrock for learning. Being able to handwrite allows children to express themselves on paper and gives them confidence as well as pride in their work. Many teachers will have seen the utter delight in children's eyes when they first discover that they can communicate through marks on the page. It is also sometimes overlooked that handwriting supports the mastery of other skills in school, such as early reading, spelling and the securing of mathematical concepts. The physical connectivity with the pencil seems to impact on the brain in a way that using a keyboard does not[1, 2]. If children can learn to write legibly, fluently and automatically when they are in the primary school, this skill then allows them to engage fully with the secondary curriculum where they are expected to take notes, produce written assignments in class, and complete tests and exams under timed conditions[3]. Being able to fully demonstrate understanding, knowledge and ability is critical to their progress as this is the way in which they are judged. It is important that handwriting has been *fully* mastered as it has been demonstrated in several research studies that failing to write legibly can cost vital marks in tests and exams where examiners struggle to read the text[4]. It has also been found that where young people cannot get enough work down on the page, the content of what they write suffers[5, 6, 7]. In these ways, handwriting has been shown to play a vital role in academic success at school.

Where schools equip themselves with a scheme, such as *Penpals for Handwriting*, which supports statutory curriculum requirements, they can promote excellence in handwriting and benefit from its application across the curriculum.

Dr Angela Webb,
Chair of The National Handwriting Association

[1] Anthony et al, 2007
[2] James et al, 2015
[3] Muller & Oppenheimer, 2014
[4] Santangelo & Graham, 2015
[5] Christensen, 2005
[6] Connelly et al, 2001
[7] Webb et al, 2011

Handwriting is the ultimate fine motor task, which additionally requires skills in hand-eye co-ordination, organisation and sequencing. We expect these skills of very young children, all too often before they are developmentally ready, for example requiring fine motor control of fingers before having postural stability. Pre-writing skills can be learnt, but we should not expect letter and number formation until they can master an oblique cross (X), which requires crossing midline.

Many children with handwriting difficulties are referred to occupational therapists who can help improve letter formation, fluency and pencil grip, for example, but it would be of greater benefit to make sure children get the basics of handwriting correct at the outset. *Penpals for Handwriting* will help establish the right skills at the right time for each child and so make this essential communication tool a pleasure rather than a chore.

Catherine Elsey
State Registered Occupational Therapist,
National Handwriting Association

Sequence of teaching in a discrete handwriting session

The intended sequence is:

1. **Teach:** The teacher introduces the unit focus using the *Penpals* Interactive.

2. **Practise:** The child practises the unit focus through a short activity or text. There is generally no additional cognitive demand so children can concentrate on their handwriting; however, some of the units make reference to the wider curriculum.

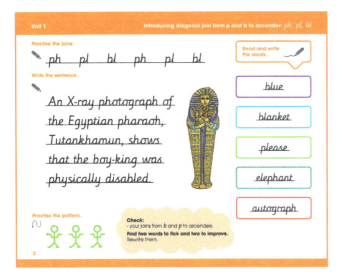

3. **Assess:** Children are asked to self- or peer-assess their handwriting.

4. **Apply:** Following a brief introduction to rehearse the join or focus, children use the Workbook in which they are asked to complete an activity where there is a cognitive demand in addition to the handwriting focus. This enables the child to apply their handwriting in a brief activity. Please note that the Workbooks should not be used to introduce a GPS concept, but should only be used for reinforcement and consolidation.

5. **Assess:** Children are asked to self- or peer-assess their handwriting as well as the GPS objective.

A note about grammar, punctuation and spelling

The revised edition of *Penpals for Handwriting* enables you to support your teaching of the grammar, spelling and punctuation curriculum with handwriting. These are all skills needed for transcribing ideas and children need to be able to combine them effortlessly.

By Year 4, most children will be refining the finer points of their handwriting and beginning to appreciate its value as a curriculum tool; they should know that we use different styles for different purposes. Combining handwriting with the cognitive demands of grammar, spelling and punctuation provides children with an 'authentic' cross-curricular handwriting experience. Ongoing discrete handwriting teaching and practice is essential.

A note about application of handwriting across the curriculum

One of the challenges of all handwriting programmes is achieving the transfer of skills from the child's handwriting book to their writing across the curriculum and in all other circumstances. The Workbooks are intended to support this transfer by offering grammar, punctuation and spelling (GPS) activities with a handwriting focus as outlined above. High frequency words, also known as common exception words, from *National Curriculum* (2014) are embedded in all the resources where it makes sense. After following the suggested teaching sequence below, transfer of the join or other unit focus into writing across the curriculum should be encouraged. Many of the Pupil Book units encourage this wider application.

Sequence of teaching in a discrete handwriting session

Ten units have been provided for each school term. The terms have been organised into a specific teaching sequence to ensure that skills are developed, practised and consolidated. Units 10, 20 and 29 are assessment units, which give both practitioner and children the opportunity to review progress and set new targets if appropriate.

For each unit, you will need:
- The Y4 Teacher's Book.
- The Y4 Interactive.
- An interactive whiteboard or tablet.
- A laptop or PC connected to a data projector.

Children will need:
- A sharp pencil and writing book each. Dry-wipe pens and small whiteboards can be used if preferred; however, since good posture is crucial to good handwriting, it is important to ensure that children are sitting at a table with both feet flat on the floor for their written work.
- Coloured pencils.
- Y4 Practice Book.
- Y4 Workbook.

The teaching sequence of each unit generally follows the common pattern outlined here.

Using the Interactives: whole-class session

1. **Unit focus:** This is clearly identified at the start of each unit.

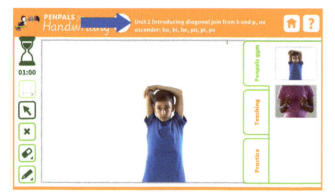

2. **Penpals gym:** Handwriting is a physical activity so children need to warm up their muscles. Use the activities shown to physically prepare the core muscles and the hands for handwriting.

3. **Teach (Letter/join animations):** These provide opportunities to talk about correct join formations and/or the specific unit focus. Children can practise palm writing and copying the letters/joins in the identified words.

4. **Teach (Gallery):** This includes samples of handwriting for children to assess. Look at some examples of good writing and identify necessary improvements in poor samples.

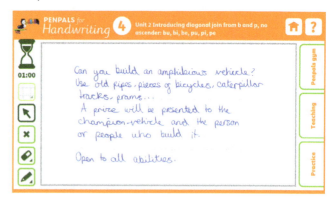

5. **Practise (Word Bank):** Model how to click a letter or word from the Word Bank to practise tracing and writing it on-screen. Invite children to engage with this in a teaching session or independently as practice.

The Word Bank includes a Challenge Word which is also provided as an image. Invite children to identify the word, which will be linked to the unit focus.

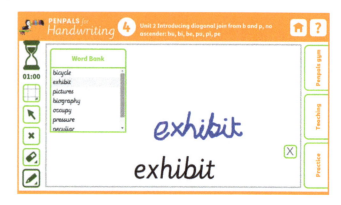

Using the Practice Book

This session should ideally follow on directly from the whole-class session. It is best if work is overseen by an adult to ensure correct letter formation and joining, especially for children about whom there are concerns. The teacher's page for the unit provides key learning points to help identify issues on which to focus.

1. **Independent writing:** Practice of the join or unit focus.

2. **Writing the unit focus, letter or join in context:** Once children have practised the joins separately, they should try to write them in a simple phrase, sentence, activity, joke or rhyme.

3. **Self- or peer-assessment:** Children are asked to identify where they have demonstrated control of the unit focus and where they need to improve. They should then improve that letter, join or word.

4. **Pattern practice:** Children will need coloured pencils, or similar, to practise the pattern at the bottom of the page. These usually reflect the pencil movement of the unit focus, but always enhance fine motor control. These patterns are artwork, not letters, and should be treated as opportunities to develop fluent and controlled movement.

Using the Workbook

Once their work has been checked, children can move directly from the Practice Book to the Workbook. The Workbooks offer an opportunity to use the handwriting join or focus to consolidate (not to teach or introduce) understanding from GPS (Grammar, Punctuation and Spelling) lessons. You may want to monitor children as they progress through this session.

If your timetable means that the Workbook activity is introduced on another day, revisit the unit on the IWB to remind children of the handwriting focus. One or more of the words in the word bank will be relevant to the Workbook session.

1. **Independent writing:** Practice of the focus join or joins.

2. **Writing joins in words or groups of letters:** Once children have practised writing the unit focus, letters or joins, they should use them in words which are relevant to the grammar, punctuation or spelling activity.

3. **Introduce the activity:** Explain the grammar, punctuation or spelling focus and talk about the activity. See the chart on p4 which provides an overview of the GPS content.

4. **Completing the activity:** Children complete the activity, following the instructions.

5. **Self- or peer-assess:** Children assess their achievement in terms of both handwriting and the grammar, punctuation and spelling focus. As before, they identify where they have managed the join or handwriting focus well and letters, joins or words to improve.

6. **Challenge activity:** There is often an additional Challenge activity, for those children who need it, to attempt.

Home practice

Photocopy masters (PCMs) are provided at the back of the teacher's book for extra practice or for homework.

Rules for handwriting

Towards the beginning of the school year, spend a handwriting lesson with your class agreeing handwriting rules. These may include, for example:

- Sit looking at the board or book.
- Sit with both feet, and all four chair legs, on the ground.
- Place your paper or small whiteboard at a comfortable angle.
- Always use a sharp pencil when you are writing.
- All the letters should sit on the line, except those which have a descender.
- Lower case letters should all be the same height, unless they have ascenders.
- Capital letters should all be the same height as ascenders.

These handwriting rules should be clearly displayed to remind children of handwriting expectations in all writing tasks.

Left-handed children

There is no reason why left-handed children should have worse handwriting than right-handed children.

Nevertheless, left-handers do have additional challenges which include pushing the pencil across the page, rather than pulling it across, and covering up their writing as they do so. The recommendation is always:

- Seat the child so that their left elbow is free to move without colliding into a right-handed child's elbow.
- Teach the child to hold their pencil between 2 and 5 centimetres from the point. This enables them to see their writing and lifts their hand away from the page.
- Encourage the left-handed child to place their paper or small whiteboard at a greater angle than you would expect for a right-handed child. The lower arm should be at a right-angle to the bottom edge of the paper.
- Establish the expectation that the hand is below the writing line and the wrist is straight – discourage children from hooking their hand round their writing.
- Left-handed children may benefit from using a writing slope to reinforce this angle.
- In general, the writing modelled in *Penpals* has a slight forwards slope which is more formally taught in Years 5 and 6. This may be hard for left-handers to achieve. However, encourage an upright letter formation and discourage a backwards slope.

Organisational issues

Classroom organisation

The ideal classroom organisation for teaching *Penpals* is to seat children at desks or tables which are arranged so that they can all see the IWB. Each child needs a sharp pencil and a writing book or a dry-wipe board, with guidelines.

If this organisation is not possible within your classroom, bear in mind the following points as you plan your own classroom:

- All children need to face the IWB and be comfortably able to copy words or handwriting patterns from it.
- Handwriting in books is usually completed on a horizontal or slightly sloping surface.

When to use *Penpals*

Penpals can be used flexibly to teach handwriting. The National Curriculum (2014) recommends that handwriting requires "frequent and discrete, direct teaching". Ideally the whole-class teaching session will be followed immediately by independent work in the Practice Book and then consolidation work in the Workbook.

Timing the sessions

The whole-class session for each unit, including the *Penpals* gym activity, should take no more than 15 minutes. The independent work session should take another 20 to 30 minutes if both the Practice Book and the Workbook are to be used, although you may choose to use the Workbook on a separate occasion.

In addition to the allocated handwriting lesson, extra daily practice times of 5 to 10 minutes are recommended, particularly for children who require handwriting support.

Differentiation

Differentiation ideas for the Practice book and Workbook are always indicated for each unit of the Teacher's Books. In addition, differentiation in *Penpals for Handwriting* can be achieved in a number of ways:

- Children working individually or in small groups with a teaching assistant may benefit from additional practice on small whiteboards.
- Some children may benefit from revisiting some of the materials in the units for the previous year to revise the teaching of the letters or joins.

- Home practice activities provide additional opportunities for differentiation since the letters and joins are often suitable for tracing.
- Challenge your higher achieving children through the challenge activities provided and more demanding targets for control and evenness of letters.

The *Penpals for Handwriting Intervention Programme* can be used for isolated additional support or as a handwriting intervention.

Assessment and record keeping

On-going formative assessment

The most effective assessment of handwriting is ongoing self-, peer- and teacher-assessment because this gives you the chance to spot any errors or inconsistencies that are likely to impede a fast, fluent handwriting style in the future *before* they become ingrained. Be particularly aware of left-handed children and prevent them from developing a hooked style that will be hard to move away from.

Formative assessment opportunities are identified in every unit using key learning points. Encourage your children to understand what is meant and assessed by these points.

Summative assessment

Beginning of year

In Y4, a 'starting point assessment' PCM is provided for use at the beginning of the school year (see p12). This assesses the previous year's work and may be used as an indication of what the child needs to consolidate before beginning new work. For a checklist for use when marking, refer to the Y3 Practice Book contents page, or the scope and sequence at the start of the Y3 Teacher's Book. Additional assessments are provided in the *Penpals for Handwriting Intervention Programme.*

If children's joining is insecure, they will benefit from revision of the previous year's materials or by using the additional practice opportunities afforded by the photocopy masters (PCMs) and the *Penpals for Handwriting Intervention Programme.*

End of term 2

Units 10 and 20 are presented as an end-of-term check in order for you to judge children's progress. In the Practice Book, children are asked to practise writing words or a brief text featuring the teaching content of the previous ten units.

In the Workbook, children are asked to recall some of the grammar, punctuation and spelling practised during the term and then to assess this along with their handwriting.

End of year

You can use the text in Unit 29 of the Practice Book as the basis of a summative assessment. It requires the children to copy a text and then to self- or peer-assess this using a checklist.

At the end of each Workbook a certificate is provided to celebrate children's completion of the year. Encourage them to write their whole name in their best handwriting and then to decorate the certificate using patterns they have practised. This is another opportunity to celebrate success and hard work.

Record keeping

The best record of what children have achieved will be in their designated handwriting exercise book and in their Workbook. It is therefore important to keep a book specifically for this purpose. It will provide a useful record of progress and achievement to share with parents and colleagues and for children to take pride in.

If you wish, the contents page of the teacher's book can be photocopied and annotated with dates to keep a record of attainment in each unit. Use 'RAG rating' (Red for 'not achieved', Amber for 'partially achieved' and Green for 'fully achieved') to identify units children need to revisit either individually or in a group.

Beginning of year assessment

Name .... Date ....

Write the words in stages, then write the whole word.

din o saur   dinosaur
_____   _____

al lig a tor   alligator
_____   _____

ele ph ant   elephant
_____   _____

rh in o cer os   rhinoceros
_____   _____

croc o dile   crocodile
_____   _____

ant e lope   antelope
_____   _____

gi raffe   giraffe
_____   _____

hip po pot a mus   hippopotamus
_____   _____

Key issues

Talking about handwriting: glossary of key terms

Throughout *Penpals for Handwriting* it has been assumed that the correct terminology should be used with children as soon as possible. During Key Stage 1, children have been used to using correct terminology and this should be continued during Key Stage 2.

Terms used in *Penpals* include:

- **Lower case letter**
- **Capital letter** is used in preference to 'upper case letter'.
- **Letter with an ascender**
- **Letter with a descender**
- **x-height letter** is used to describe a letter with no ascender or descender.
- **Break letter** – a letter that is not generally joined from. (g, y, j, f, z, x)
- **Curve** is used to describe the curved movement at the bottom of downstrokes such as t, g and the top and bottom of f.
- **Cross bar** is used to describe the left-to-right line on t and f. It may also be used in relation to letters that feature a left-to-right horizontal line (e.g. e and z).
- **Diagonal join to ascender** (e.g. *at*), **diagonal join (no ascender)** (e.g. *du*), **diagonal join to an anticlockwise letter** (e.g. *ho*)
- **Horizontal join to ascender** (e.g. *oh*), **horizontal join (no ascender)** (e.g. *re*), **horizontal join to an anticlockwise letter** (e.g. *wo*)
- Other important terminology used includes **vertical**, **parallel**, **joined**, **sloped**, **anticlockwise**.

Notes on formation of specific letters and joins

Correct letter formation can be demonstrated using the **Show alphabet** section on the interactives.

- k The use of the curly form of k, as opposed to the straight k, is recommended by handwriting experts because its flowing form lends itself more naturally to joining. It is also more easily distinguished from the capital letter.
- o, v and w There is no exit stroke from the lower case o, v and w when it is not joined. Unlike the flick at the bottom of letters like n and l, the exit stroke from the o, v and w is not an integral part of the letter but simply a mechanism for joining.
- e Two different forms of e (i.e. e and e) are used in order to show children how it alters when other letters are joined to it.
- g, j and y are letters that do not join.
- x and z are never joined to or from other letters as these are uncomfortable joins that often result in

the malformation of both the joining letter and the x or z. Also, handwriting is generally faster and more legible if it is not continuously joined. In the interests of developing a personalised style, there is some exploration of joining g, j, y, x and z and of alternative ways to join f, t, b and s in Year 6.

Capital letters

It is generally agreed that there is no right or wrong way to form capitals; however, we suggest they should be written from top to bottom and left to right wherever possible as skills and confidence develop. Left-handers may well form capitals differently – they have a tendency to go from right to left, for example; this should not be an issue as capitals are never joined.

Spacing between words

The use of 'finger spaces' in writing is tricky and contentious, but important. Many young children, and some older children still struggling with writing, have difficulty processing the notion that after each word there should be a space. They need to be encouraged to verbalise what it is they are writing and then physically respond in some way, with a finger tap after each word perhaps, to remind them that this means they need to leave a space in their writing.

When they understand this notion, then we can begin to teach the refinement of how big the space should be; with young children we sometimes demonstrate this by using a finger and suggesting it is a finger space. Although note that left-handed children should never be asked to use their own fingers for finger spacing because it is impracticable and always impedes writing. Quite quickly children should understand that the ideal space between words should be no wider than one or two of their own letter os.

Letter spacing within a word is also increasingly important. The spacing around each letter should be broadly even and regular. If children's writing begins to look cramped, check that their letter formation is correct and later that their joining lines are long enough. Check also that the child's writing arm is not tight in to their sides as the elbow needs room to move about if writing is ultimately to be fast and fluent.

At key points in their handwriting journey spacing will need to be revisited. Each new join needs extra practice and once they are confidently experimenting with slope and a personalised style, children should also be confident enough to observe and respond to any new challenges that arise around spacing issues as a result of new handwriting choices made.

Handwriting policy

The following content provides a short example of a handwriting policy that you may wish to adapt and use for your own school. An editable version of this content can be found at education.cambridge.org/penpalswelcome.

We aim for our children to leave in Year 6 with the ability to write using their own style of fast, fluent, legible and sustainable handwriting, as well as other styles of writing for specific purposes. In addition to teaching handwriting during our regular handwriting lessons, we have high expectations that what is taught and practiced in handwriting lessons will be used in all writing activities. We believe that handwriting is integral to a child's personal development and know that children's engagement and self-esteem can be improved by their satisfaction and pride in good quality presentation.

Aims

Handwriting is a taught skill that develops at different rates for different children. All of the teachers in the school put a priority on teaching handwriting and have high expectations for handwriting across the curriculum. Our school uses *Penpals for Handwriting* to ensure that:

- The importance of handwriting is recognised and given appropriate time.
- The progression of handwriting is consistent across the school.
- Handwriting is acknowledged to be a whole body activity and emphasis is placed on correct posture and pencil grip for handwriting.
- Expectations of left-handed children are equal to those of right-handed children, and appropriate advice and resources are available to ensure that they learn to write with a comfortable, straight wrist.
- Handwriting is linked into grammar, punctuation and spelling in order to practice and contextualise all of the transcriptional and stylistic skills for writing.
- Children learn to self-assess their own writing and develop understanding and responsibility for improving it.
- Children learn to write in different styles for different purposes such as print for labelling a diagram, illustrated capitals letters for creating a poster, swift jottings for writing notes, making a 'best copy' for presentation and fast, fluent and legible writing across the curriculum.

Progression of skills

Penpals enables us to teach and secure the development of handwriting throughout the school:

- First, children experience the foundation of handwriting through multi-sensory activities (EYFS F1 and F2).
- Correct letter formation is taught, practised, applied and consolidated (EYFS F2/Y1).
- Joining is introduced only after correct letter formation is used automatically (Y1/Y2/Y3).

- Joins are introduced systematically and cumulatively (Y2–Y6).
- As children practice joining, they pay attention to the size, proportion and spacing of their letters and words (Y3–Y6).
- Once the joins are secure, a slope is introduced in order to support increased speed and fluency (Y5).
- Children are introduced to different ways of joining in order that they can develop their own preferred personal style (Y6).

In using *Penpals*, we ensure that our children follow the requirements and recommendations of the National Curriculum. We share the aspirations that children's handwriting should be 'sufficiently fluent and effortless for them to manage the general demands of the curriculum' and that 'problems with forming letters do not get in the way of their writing down what they want to say'.

Handwriting tools

Throughout their time in school, children use a range of tools for different purposes and styles of handwriting including:

- A wide range of tools and media for mark-making in the EYFS.
- Whiteboard pens throughout the school.
- Fingers when writing on the interactive whiteboard.
- Art supplies including coloured pens and pencils for posters, displays and artwork.
- Sharp pencils for most writing until a pen licence is awarded.
- A handwriting pen for when they sustain a good level of presentation.

Handwriting is always introduced and practised in the *Penpals* Practice Books and on lined paper so that children quickly learn about letter orientation including ascenders and descenders. As children's fine motor skills improve and their letter formation or joining becomes increasingly accurate, the width between the lines they write on gradually decreases.

Equality of opportunity

All of our children have equal access to handwriting lessons and to the resources available. We recognise that some children take longer to develop the necessary skills and we cater for those children by providing additional opportunities for skills development. Children who need specific fine motor or handwriting interventions are identified early and the impact of interventions is carefully monitored. Children with a physical disability are catered for, and progress is monitored, according to their individual action plans.

Joining

Penpals for Handwriting F1, F2 and Year 1 introduce, practise and consolidate letter formation in letter families.

By the time they reach the Year 3 resources, children should be becoming secure and confident with the common joins and beginning to use them in all 'neat' writing activities. The emphasis throughout *Penpals* is on developing a fluent and even handwriting style, ensuring consistency in the size and proportion of letters, in the spaces between and within words and in parallel downstrokes.

Progression in the introduction of joins

Y1/P2

In order to support the early stages of spelling, some joins are introduced in the final term of Year 1. In paired units, children practise writing the letters and then practise joining pairs of letters. The range of *Penpals* resources support a gradual progression from practising joins in isolation, to joining pairs of letters in words.

- Children should be taught to:
  - sit correctly at a table, holding a pencil comfortably and correctly
  - begin to form lower case letters in the correct direction, starting and finishing in the right place
  - form capital letters
  - form the digits 0 to 9
  - understand which letters belong to which handwriting families (i.e. letters that are formed in similar ways) and to practise these. (*National Curriculum 2014*)
- Throughout Year 1, reinforce a good pencil grip and correct letter formation in all writing that children do.
- Throughout the year, children's motor skills will improve and become more precise. Correct letter formation should become an automatic habit.
- Don't make children write too small or too quickly. As with most aspects of their development, children's ability to manipulate pencils will mature at different ages. Trying to enforce small handwriting too soon can lead to a very cramped style which is then difficult to make fluent.

Y2/P3

During Year 2, all of the basic joins are taught. Until the summer term, there is no expectation that children will automatically join letters they have not been explicitly taught, although this should be encouraged if children begin to explore. For example, the movement for the join *wh* (i.e. horizontal join to ascender) is exactly the same as for joining *oh*, *ol*, *ot*, *ob* and so on.

Once a join has been introduced between pairs of letters (e.g. *wh*), children will always be expected to copy the model showing those joined letter pairs. In this way,

children are gradually introduced to the idea of joining more than one pair of letters within a word.

In the final term of Year 2, children are introduced to other pairs of letters which are joined using the same joining strokes.

Pupils should be taught to:

- form lower case letters of the correct size relative to one another
- start using some of the diagonal and horizontal strokes needed to join letters and understand which letters, when adjacent to one another, are best left unjoined
- write capital letters and digits of the correct size, orientation and relationship to one another and to lower case letters
- use spacing between words that reflects the size of the letters.

Y3/P4 and Y4/P5

From Year 3, when all of the basic joins have all been taught and practised, you should begin to encourage joined writing across the curriculum. Use the *Penpals for Handwriting Intervention Programme* to reinforce inaccurate or messy joins.

During Years 3 and 4, children are introduced to the idea of joining through a word and to trickier joins such as joining from *r*, *s* and *f*. Additionally they learn how to join from *p* and *b*.

As the movement for joins becomes more familiar and fluent, the focus moves to develop a neat and even style by looking at size and proportion, parallel downstrokes and spacing.

Pupils should be taught to:

- use the diagonal and horizontal strokes that are needed to join letters and understand which letters, when adjacent to one another, are best left unjoined
- increase the legibility, consistency and quality of their handwriting (e.g. by ensuring that the downstrokes of letters are parallel and equidistant).

Y5/P6

In Year 5 a slightly more sloped style is introduced to enable speedier writing. All previous taught letters and joins are revisited to enable children to practise the slope in familiar contexts. Children focus on issues of proportion, size, legibility and different styles for different purposes.

Children revisit and reinforce all of the joins to build increased speed and fluency using a sloped style of handwriting. Many children will now be writing primarily in pen.

Joining

In Years 5 and 6, pupils should be taught to:

- write legibly, fluently and with increasing speed by:
  - choosing which shape of a letter to use when given choices and deciding whether or not to join specific letters
  - choosing the writing implement that is best suited for a task.

Y6/P7

The emphasis should now be on developing a personal, fast, fluent and legible handwriting style. Children are given opportunities to practise a range of ways of joining with the expectation that they will develop a style that 'works' for them. Additionally, children continue to focus on key issues for legibility and speed as well as styles and implements for different purposes.

Defining the joins

(See p17 of this Teacher's Book for a full list of letter sets requiring each of the joins as taught in Year 4.)

The two basic join types

- **Diagonal join** (e.g. *at*) (introduced in Year 1/Primary 2, Unit 23): This is the most common join. It starts from the final flick on the baseline (or 'curl' in the case of the letter t).
- **Horizontal join** (e.g. *wh*) (introduced in Year 1/Primary 2, Unit 27): This join is formed from letters that finish at the top of the letter rather than at the baseline.

Variations on the join types

Penpals uses three subsets of the main joins: join to a letter with an ascender, join to a letter with no ascender and join to a letter that begins with an anticlockwise movement. Since the last subset involves stopping the pencil and reversing the direction of movement, these are called 'diagonal join to an anticlockwise letter' and 'horizontal join to an anticlockwise letter'. Joins to anticlockwise letters are trickier to teach and need more practice than straightforward horizontal and diagonal joins. These joins tend to 'decay' when children begin to write more quickly.

- **Diagonal join to a letter with an ascender** (e.g. *ch*) (introduced in Year 1/Primary 2, Unit 23): This is a variation of the diagonal join.
- **Horizontal join to a letter with an ascender** (e.g. *wh*) (introduced in Year 1/Primary 2, Unit 27) This is a variation of the horizontal join.
- **Diagonal join to an anticlockwise letter** (e.g. *ea*) (introduced in Year 2/Primary 3, Unit 11): Joining with a diagonal join to the anticlockwise letters in the 'curly caterpillar' family involves stopping the hand

movement and reversing it. This can be a tricky join and it decays easily in fast writing.
- **Horizontal join to an anticlockwise letter** (e.g. *oo*) (introduced in Year 2/Primary 3, Unit 14): Joining from a horizontal join to an anticlockwise letter involves a reversal in the direction of the pencil movement.
- **Break letters** (introduced in Year 3/Primary 4, Unit 10): These are letters from which no join has yet been taught (see notes on p13).

Correct formation of key joins can be demonstrated using the **Library of joins** section in the interactives.

Joining for Year 4

Diagonal join to ascender (e.g. *at*)
This join is used to join letters in this box . . .

> a b c d e h i k l m n p s t u

to letters in this box.

> b f h k l t

Diagonal join, no ascender (e.g. *da*)
This join is used to join letters in this box . . .

> a b c d e h i k l m n p q s t u

to letters in this box.

> e i j m n p r u v w y
>
> *a c d g o q s

Horizontal join, no ascender (e.g. *wo*)
This join is used to join letters in this box . . .

> f o r v w

to letters in this box.

> e i j m n p r u v w y
>
> *a c d g o q s

Horizontal join to ascender (e.g. *oh*)
This join is used to join letters in this box . . .

> f o r v w

to letters in this box.

> b f h k l t

Break letters
Joins are not made from these letters.

> g j y

Joins are not made to or from these letters.

> x z

* anticlockwise letters

17

Key learning

- Introducing joining from *p* and *b* to ascender. Check the curve of *p* and *b* touches the upright line before the join begins.
- Ascenders are equal height.
- All familiar joins are used. Break letters are now *g, y, j, x, z*.

1   Using the Interactives

Penpals gym

- Ask children to try the warm-ups: **Curved back** and **Clasp and grasp**, or choose others from the reference area.

Teach

- Demonstrate the animated joins. Children should practise these. Ensure the curve of *p* and *b* touches the upright line before beginning the join.
- Look at the examples of children's work. Ask children to identify and assess the target joins.

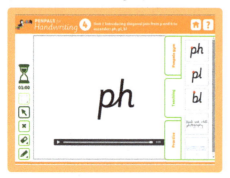

Practise

- Children practise the pattern and use the word bank: *people, photograph, phone, planet, blanket, blind, blue, disabled*.
- The challenge word is *photograph*.

2   Using the Practice Book (p2)

a   Watch while children write the joins. Check the key learning points above.

b   Read the text together and identify the joins from *p* and *b*. Then children write the text.

c   Children read each word before writing it to practise the *p* and *b* joins.

d   Self- or peer-assess: ask children to identify their best joins from *p* and *b*, finding one of each to tick and one of each to improve.

e   Children finger trace and write the pattern.

3   Using the Workbook (p2)

Handwriting practice with a grammar focus: noun phrases

a   Watch while children write the new joins. Check the key learning points.

b   Watch them write the words in the noun phrase. Check the new and known joins.

c   Revisit rules for using adjectives to noun phrases. Ask children to complete the noun phrases.

d   Challenge activity: write a new noun phrase using *b* and *p* joins to ascender.

e   Self- or peer-assess: ask children to check the sentences, finding two words to tick and two to improve.

4   Extra support

Small group work: Practice Book

- Ensure children can consistently write *p* and *b* joins to ascender correctly before moving on. If necessary, draw lines showing where the ascenders/descenders should reach.
- Read the text together before children write it. Or they can just write words with *b* or *p* joins to ascender.

Small group work: Workbook

- Pre-teach the individual joins: *ph, pl, bl* with a focus on the ascender height and descender length.
- Read the noun phrase together. Children find the joins *pl* and *ph* and then write those words and then the text.
- Ask children work to together to say and write a noun phrase with a focus on the joins from *p* and *b*.

Homework

- PCM 1 on page 48.

5   Common errors

- The curve of *p* and *b* does not touch the upright stroke before the join begins.
- The join line is too short or too long resulting in uneven spacing between letters.
- Ascenders and descenders are not parallel.

Unit 2   Introducing diagonal join from p and b, no ascender: *bu, bi, be, pu, pi, pe*

Key learning

- Introducing joining from **p** and **b**, no ascender.
- Ascenders and descenders are parallel.
- The curve of **p** and **b** must touch the upright stroke before the join begins.

1   Using the Interactives

Penpals gym

- Ask children to try the warm-ups: **Underarm stretch** and **Finger point**, or choose others from the reference area.

Teach

- Demonstrate the animated joins. Children should practise these.
- Look at the examples of children's work. Ask children to identify and assess the target joins.

Practise

- Children practise the pattern and use the word bank: *bicycle, exhibit, pictures, biography, occupy, pressure, peculiar, amphibious*.
- The challenge word is *bicycle*.

2   Using the Practice Book (p3)

a   Watch while children write the joins. Check the key learning points above.

b   Read the text together and identify the joins from **p** and **b**. Then children write the text.

c   Children read each word before writing it to practise the **p** and **b** joins.

d   Self- or peer-assess: ask children to identify their best joins from **p** and **b**, finding one of each to tick and one of each to improve.

e   Children finger trace and write the pattern, focusing on making height consistent.

3   Using the Workbook (p3)

Handwriting practice with a spelling focus: prefixes *bio–, bi–*

a   Watch while children write the new joins. Check the key learning points.

b   Discuss the meaning of each prefix ('bio' = life, 'bi' = two). Revise rules for making words using word webs.

c   Ask children to write two sentences using some of the words they have made.

d   Self- or peer-assess: ask children to check the words, finding two new joins to tick and two to improve.

4   Extra support

Small group work: Practice Book

- Practise **p** and **b** joins until they are accurate. If necessary, draw lines to show where ascenders/descenders should reach.
- Read the text together before children write it all. Or they can just write words with joins from **b** or **p**.

Small group work: Workbook

- Practise the individual joins.
- Model completing the word webs. Talk about word meanings.
- Children work together to think of sentences and then write them with a focus on joins from **p** and **b**.

Homework

- PCM 2 on page 48.

5   Common errors

- The curve of **p** and **b** doesn't touch the upright before the join begins.
- The join line is too short or too long resulting in uneven spacing between letters.
- Ascenders and descenders are not parallel.

Unit 3 Introducing diagonal join from *p* and *b* to an anticlockwise letter: *pa, po, ps, ba, bo, bs*

Key learning

- Introducing joining from *p* and *b*, to anticlockwise.
- Ascenders and descenders are parallel.
- The curve of *p* and *b* must touch the upright stroke before the join begins.

1 Using the Interactives

Penpals gym

- Ask children to try the warm-ups: **Stretch** and **Parallel lines**, or choose others from the reference area.

Teach

- Demonstrate the animated joins. Children should practise these.
- Look at the examples of children's work. Ask children to identify and assess the target joins.

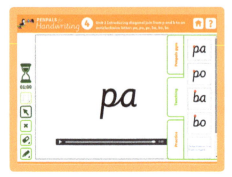

Practise

- Children practise the pattern and use the word bank: *basket, probably, embarrass, separate, popular, potato, perhaps, impatient*.
- The challenge word is *basket*.

2 Using the Practice Book (p4)

a Watch while children write the joins. Check the key learning points above.

b Read the index together and identify the joins from *p* and *b* . Discuss text layout before children write the text.

c Children add two more animals to their index and then write a title for the book.

d Children read each word before writing it.

e Self- or peer-assess: ask children to identify their best joins from *p* and *b*, finding one of each to tick and one of each to improve.

f Children finger trace and write the pattern.

3 Using the Workbook (p4)

Handwriting practice with a spelling focus: adverbials

a Watch while children write the new joins. Check *a* and *o* are closed and letter shapes are not distorted.

b Watch them write the words. Check the key learning points.

c Revisit the meaning of each adverbial. Ask children to complete the sentences.

d Challenge activity: Children write their own sentence using *possibly*.

e Self- or peer-assess: ask children to check the sentences, finding one two words to tick and two to improve.

4 Extra support

Small group work: Practice Book

- Practise *p* and *b* joins until they are accurate. If necessary, draw lines to show where ascenders/descenders should reach.
- Read the index together discussing its purpose and layout, before children write it.

Small group work: Workbook

- Practise the individual joins with a focus on letter formation and closing letters.
- Ask children to identify joins from *b* and *p* and then write the words.
- Ask children to work together to decide how to complete the sentences. Then they write them with a focus on joins from *p* and *b*.

Homework

- PCM 3 on page 49.

5 Common errors

- The curve of p and b doesn't touch the upright before the join begins.
- The join line is too short or too long resulting in uneven spacing between letters.
- Ascenders and descenders are not parallel.

Key learning

- Revising parallel ascenders and descenders.
- The curve of *p* and *b* must touch the upright stroke before the join begins.

1 Using the Interactives

Penpals gym

- Ask children to try the warm-ups: **Bend and push** and **Hand clap**, or choose others from the reference area.

Teach

- Discuss the text. Children identify the key *pp* and *bb* joins and then practise these.
- Look at the examples of children's work. Ask children to identify and assess the target joins.

Practise

- Children practise the pattern and use the word bank: *bubble*, *puppet*, *cabbage*, *happened*, *clapped*, *stubborn*, *disappear*, *applause*.
- The challenge word is *bubble*.

2 Using the Practice Book (p5)

a Watch while children write the joins. Check the key learning points above.

b Watch while children write the sentence. Check parallel ascenders and descenders.

c Read the main clauses together and talk about how they might be continued. Children write the clauses and then add a new clause to each.

d Children read each word before writing it.

e Self- or peer-assess: ask children to identify their best *pp* and their best *bb*, finding one of each to tick and one of each to improve.

f Children finger trace and write the pattern, focusing on parallel lines.

3 Using the Workbook (p5)

Handwriting practice with a spelling focus: suffixes –*ing*, –*ed*, –*er*

a Watch while children write the new joins. Check parallel ascenders and descenders.

b Revisit the meaning of each verb inflection. Revise spelling rules. Ask children to complete the table.

c Challenge activity: ask children to write a sentence containing one word with *pp* and one with *bb*.

d Self- or peer-assess: ask children to check the sentences, finding two words to tick and two to improve.

4 Extra support

Small group work: Practice Book

- Practice *pp* and *bb* joins. If necessary, draw lines to show where ascenders/descenders should reach.
- Read the text together and discuss ways to finish the sentences, before children write the whole sentences.

Small group work: Workbook

- Practice the joins with a focus on parallel ascenders and descenders.
- Model completing the table. Find the *pp* and *bb* joins. Children work independently to fill in the words.
- Ask children to work together to think of sentences and then to write them with a focus on parallel ascenders and descenders.

Homework

- PCM 4 on page 49.

5 Common errors

- The curve of *p* and *b* doesn't touch the upright.
- Ascenders and descenders are not parallel.
- Uneven spacing between letters.

Unit 5   Break letters: x, z

Key learning

- Break letters are: **g, y, j, x, z**. All other letters should be joined.
- Spacing between letters is regular.
- Join to **z** but not from it. Don't join to or from **x**.

1   Using the Interactives

Penpals gym

- Ask children to try the warm-ups: **Head roll** and **Blindfold**, or choose others from the reference area.

Teach

- Discuss the text on screen. Establish the use of break letters in the sentence. Children should practise using pen breaks in this context.
- Look at the examples of children's work. Ask children to identify and assess the target break letters used.

Practise

- Children practise the pattern and use the word bank: **prize, dozen, exercise, beeswax, exaggerate, experiment, capsized, amazing**.
- The challenge word is **prize**.

2   Using the Practice Book (p6)

a   Watch while children write the letters. Check the key learning points above.

b   Read the text together. Can children use the picture and text to work out the meaning of *zygodactyl*? (It refers to the arrangement of toes on a parrot.)

c   Watch while children write the text. Check their spaces before and after the break letter as well as through the rest of the word.

d   Children read each word before writing it to practise spacing and break letters.

e   Self- or peer-assess: ask children to find their best two words to tick and two to improve.

f   Children finger trace and write the pattern, focusing on regular spacing.

3   Using the Workbook (p6)

Handwriting practice with a spelling focus: prefix **ex–**

a   Watch while children write the letters. Check key learning points.

b   Talk about the words from the word web. Watch children write the words. Check letter spacing within each word.

c   Revise the earlier teaching to determine the word class of a word. Remind children that some words can be both nouns and verbs (e.g. **experience**). Ask children to complete the table.

d   Challenge activity: write four words featuring **z** and **zz**.

e   Self- or peer-assess: ask children to check the sentences, finding two words to tick and two to improve.

4   Extra support

Small group work: Practice Book

- Children practise all the break letters.
- Read and discuss the text. Identify words with break letters. Children can write those before copying the text.

Small group work: Workbook

- Practise the letters shown.
- Model making the words. Discuss their meanings, and decide where each should go in the table. Then children write the words in the table.

Homework

- PCM 5 on page 50.

5   Common errors

- Looping used to join from some break letters.
- Inaccurate joining means spacing between letters is irregular.

Unit 6 Spacing in common exception words

Key learning

- Consistent spacing between letters.
- All familiar joins are accurate.

1 Using the Interactives

Penpals gym

- Ask children to try the warm-ups: **Hands and arms** and **Interlocking rings**, or choose others from the reference area.

Teach

- Discuss the text and the letter spacing within the words. Talk about the importance of consistent spacing between letters.

Practise

- Children practise the pattern and use the word bank: *interest*, *possible*, *women*, *believe*, *length*, *suppose*, *therefore*, *surprise*, *grammar*.
- The challenge word is *length*.

2 Using the Practice Book (p7)

a Read the words together and discuss meanings.
b Children write the words. Check the key learning points.
c Ask children to work in pairs to create their sentence using at least three of the exception words.
d Children read each word before writing it.
e Self- or peer-assess: ask children to find their best two words to tick and two to improve.
f Children finger trace and write the pattern, focusing on regular spacing.

3 Using the Workbook (p7)

Handwriting practice with a punctuation focus: inverted commas ("speech marks")

a Watch while children write the sentence. Check punctuation and key learning points.
b Revise punctuating direct speech. Encourage children to rehearse what they will write. Ask children to rewrite the joke as direct speech, with correct punctuation.
c Challenge activity: children use the boxes at the bottom of the page to count how many of each punctuation mark they have used.
d Self- or peer-assess: ask children to check the sentences, finding two words with consistent spacing to tick and two to improve.

4 Extra support

Small group work: Practice Book

- Read the words together and talk about meanings. Ask children to say a sentence for each word.
- Suggest children write two words at a time before checking and improving them.

Small group work: Workbook

- Children practise writing the initial sentence, with correct punctuation. Review spacing.
- Revisit the rules for punctuating direct speech.
- Ask children to say what they will write before they write the joke, starting each speaker on a new line.
- Together, add the punctuation and words to show direct speech.

Homework

- PCM 6 on page 50.

5 Common errors

- Spacing between letters is not even.
- Some joining lines are too short or too long.

Unit 7 Consistent size of letters

Key learning

- Focus on the relative size of letters, i.e. lower case letters should be the same height except for ascenders and descenders.
- *e* and *s* are the same size as *x*.

1 Using the Interactives

Penpals gym

- Ask children to try the warm-ups: **Shoulder moves** and **Knuckles, wrists and palms**, or choose others from the reference area.

Teach

- Discuss the text and the consistent size of letters within the words. Talk about the importance of consistent sizing of letters.
- Look at the examples of children's work. Ask children to identify and assess the consistency of letter size.

Practise

- Children practise the pattern and use the word bank: *parallel*, *lower case*, *perfect*, *relative*, *consistent*, *ascender*, *descender*, *handwriting*.
- The challenge word is *handwriting*.

2 Using the Practice Book (p8)

a Read the phrases in the checklist together. Check children know what each phrase means.

b Children write the heading and then the phrases. Check the key learning points above.

c Ask children to look through their recent curriculum work and mark their own writing using the checklist.

d Children read each word before writing it.

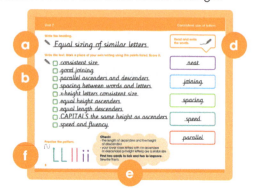

e Self- or peer-assess: ask children to find their best two words to tick and two to improve.

f Children finger trace and write the pattern, focusing on the relative size of lines.

3 Using the Workbook (p8)

Handwriting practice with a spelling focus: prefixes *in–*, *im–*, *il–*, *ir–*

a Watch while children write the prefixes. Check key learning points.

b Revise the rules that determine which prefix to add. Children complete the chart.

c Challenge activity: answer the question about the effect of the prefix.

d Self- or peer-assess: ask children to check the words for consistent size, finding two words to tick and two to improve.

4 Extra support

Small group work: Practice Book

- Read the phrases together. Talk about the meaning of each. Ask children to identify a word in their own writing which demonstrates each of the principles.
- Suggest children write the heading and then a phrase at a time before checking and improving them.

Small group work: Workbook

- Ask children to trace and write the prefixes and the words in the table.
- Together, follow the rules to decide which prefix should be added to each word and discuss the resulting change in meaning. Model completing the table.
- Children write the words using the agreed prefixes.

Homework

- PCM 7 on page 51.

5 Common errors

- Lower case letters are not consistently x-height.
- Length of ascenders and descenders is out of proportion or inconsistent.

Unit 8   Relative size of capitals

Key learning

- Capital letters are the same height as ascenders.
- Other letters are x-height except for ascenders and descenders which are the same length.

1   Using the Interactives

Penpals gym

- Ask children to try the warm-ups: **Arms high** and **Rotating wrists**, or choose others from the reference area.

Teach

- Discuss the poster text and the consistent size of capital letters used. Talk about the importance of consistent sizing of capital letters.
- Look at the examples of children's work. Ask children to identify and assess the consistency of capital letter size.

Practise

- Children practise the pattern and use the word bank: *Paris*, *Lisbon*, *Madrid*, *Berlin*, *Rome*, *Athens*.
- The challenge word is *Paris*.

2   Using the Practice Book (p9)

a   Children write the alphabet in capitals.
b   Read the poster together. Children write the poster text. Check the key learning points above.
c   Children read each word before writing it.
d   Self- or peer-assess: ask children to find their best two words to tick and two to improve.
e   Children finger trace and write the pattern, focusing on consistent line length.

3   Using the Workbook (p9)

Handwriting practice with a punctuation focus: possessive apostrophes

a   Watch while children write the sentence. Check key learning points. Talk about the need for capitals and the placement of the apostrophe.
b   Talk about where capitals are needed. Revise placement of possessive apostrophes following singular and plural nouns. Model writing the first sentence correctly. Children trace and then write the text, correcting capitals and adding apostrophes.
c   Self- or peer-assess: ask children to check the words for consistency of size of capitals, finding two words to tick and two to improve.

4   Extra support

Small group work: Practice Book

- Check formation and size of capitals.
- Talk about the poster. Point out the use of capitals and discuss their relative size. If necessary, draw lines to show the height of capitals and ascenders.
- Ask children to write the poster text.

Small group work: Workbook

- Ask children to trace and write the initial sentence.
- Remind children about rules for possessive apostrophes and model correcting the punctuation. Then children trace and write the other sentences.

Homework

- PCM 8 on page 51.

5   Common errors

- Capital letters incorrectly formed.
- Height of capitals and ascenders is irregular.
- x-height letters not a consistent size.

Unit 9 Speed and fluency

1 Using the Interactives

Penpals gym

- Ask children to try the warm-ups: **Fold and stretch** and **Quick and slow**, or choose others from the reference area.

Teach

- Discuss the poem displayed and the handwriting fluency. Ask children to practise writing the poem in a fast and fluent style.
- Look at the examples of children's work. Ask children to assess the pieces of text. Is the writing clear and legible?

Practise

- Children practise the pattern and use the word bank: *pronoun, they, theirs, him, his, us, ours, nouns, naturalist, programme, viewers*.
- The challenge word is *pronoun*.

2 Using the Practice Book (p10)

a Children write the heading.
b Children read the poem then write it neatly. Check key learning points above. Then give them 3 minutes to write as much of the poem as they can. Re-check the key learning points above.
c Children read each word before writing.

d Self- or peer-assess: ask children to count the number of words they wrote in 3 minutes, and then to find their best two words to tick and two to improve.
e Children finger trace and write the pattern, neatly, then at speed.

3 Using the Workbook (p10)

Handwriting practice with a grammar focus: personal and possessive pronouns

a Revisit the function of pronouns in sentences. Discuss the table before children trace and complete, writing quickly and fluently. Check key learning points.
b Challenge activity: children write a sentence using all three different types of pronouns.
c Self- or peer-assess: ask children to check the work against the given criteria, finding two words to tick and two to improve.

4 Extra support

Small group work: Practice Book

- Together, revisit the key learning points above.
- Read the text aloud to children.
- Children copy the text for 3 minutes, writing neatly, then repeat at speed.
- Check the accuracy of their copying and discuss how their writing changes.

Small group work: Workbook

- Revisit pronouns.
- Together, complete the table as a model.
- Children copy, writing fluently.
- Check the accuracy of their copying.

Homework

- PCM 9 on page 52.

5 Common errors

- Writing becomes illegible at speed.
- Letters such as *y* and *u* are not open and those such as *g*, *a*, *b* and *p* are not closed.
- Joins are not always correctly formed.
- Spacing between letters and words is not regular.

Unit 10   End-of-term check

Key learning

- Focus on consistent relative size of all letters.
- Take care with spacing between letters.
- Parallel ascenders and descenders.
- All letters should be joined except break letters *g, y, j, x, z*.
- All letters are correctly formed.

1 Using the Practice Book (p11)

a Read the poem together.

b Ask children to write the text. You may opt to time them. Check the key learning points above.

c Children read each word before writing it.

d Self- or peer-assess: ask children to count the number of words they wrote.

e Children finger trace and write the pattern, focusing on size and spacing.

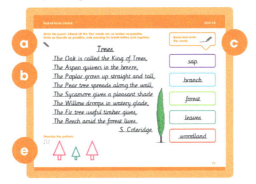

2 Using the Workbook (p11)

a Remind children to look back through the Workbook if they are unclear of the answers to any of the end-of-term check questions. Ask children to trace and answer the questions, writing quickly and fluently.

b Self- or peer-assess: ask children to mark their own work or each other's work.

3 Extra support

Small group work: Practice Book

- Read text aloud to children and discuss.
- Together, revisit the key learning points above.
- Children copy the text for 5 minutes.
- Check the accuracy of their copying.
- Help children to assess their writing and identify personal targets.

Small group work: Workbook

- Look at each question together, working out the answers before children complete the activity independently.
- Check the accuracy of children's writing.
- Children should work with a partner to mark and score their work.

Homework

- PCM 10 on page 52.

Unit 11   Revising parallel ascenders

Key learning

- Clear, legible writing at speed.
- Ascenders should be parallel and aligned with the uprights in letters like *n* and *r*.

1   Using the Interactives

Penpals gym

- Ask children to try the warm-ups: **Circles** and **Fist to fist**, or choose others from the reference area.

Teach

- Discuss the text on screen. Establish what the words *parallel* and *proportion* mean in this context.
- Look at the examples of children's work. Ask children to identify and assess the height and proportion of ascenders.

Practise

- Children practise the pattern and use the word bank: *astronaut*, *dark matter*, *meteorite*, *black hole*, *experimental*, *fascinated*, *scientist*, *constellation*.
- The challenge word is *astronaut*.

2   Using the Practice Book (p12)

a Ask children to practise the joins. Check the key learning points above.

b Children read the text and establish its context. They write the text, focusing on a fluent handwriting style with parallel ascenders.

c Children read each word before writing it.

d Self- or peer-assess: ask children to find their best two words to tick and two to improve.

e Children finger trace and write the pattern, focusing on straight, parallel lines.

3   Using the Workbook (p12)

Handwriting practice with a spelling focus: common exception words

a Children trace and write the letters. Check key learning points.

b Then children trace and write the words. Revisit the idea that parallel ascenders do not have to be neighbours and that all of the upright strokes in a word should be parallel.

c Children complete the cloze activity, writing the words in the gaps.

d Self- or peer-assess: ask children to check the words against the given criteria, finding two words to tick and two to improve.

4   Extra support

Small group work: Practice Book

- Together, revisit the key learning points.
- Ask children to write the letter pairs. Check whether they can say if the ascenders are parallel.
- Read the text aloud to children.
- Children copy the text for 5 minutes.
- Check the accuracy of their copying and discuss key learning points.

Small group work: Workbook

- Children trace and write the pairs of letters. Help them to check that ascenders are parallel.
- Talk about the silent letter in the *sc* spelling.
- Together, read the cloze and agree which is the best word each time.
- Ask children to trace and complete the sentences.

Homework

- PCM 11 on page 53.

5   Common errors

- Ascenders and other upright strokes are not parallel.
- Ascenders are out of proportion to other letters or not all the same height.
- Spacing between letters is irregular.

Unit 12   Revising parallel ascenders and break letters

Key learning

- All letters joined except break letters *g, y, j*.
- No joins to or from *x* or *z*.
- Ascenders parallel and aligned with the uprights in letters like *n* and *r*.
- Spacing is regular between letters and between words.

1   Using the Interactives

Penpals gym

- Ask children to try the warm-ups: **Backwards bends** and **Clap and grasp**, or choose others from the reference area.

Teach

- Discuss the alliterative texts. Ring the break letters. Identify parallel uprights.
- Look at the examples of children's work. Work with children to identify and assess the key learning points.

Practise

- Children practise the pattern and use the word bank: *liquid, solid, magnifying glass, observation, project file, objection, bubbles, deep freeze.*
- The challenge phrase is *liquid*.

2   Using the Practice Book (p13)

a   Children write the heading. Check they do not try to join to or from the *x, z* or capital letters. Check the key learning points above.
b   Children read the text and identify the break letters. Then ask them to write the text, focusing on a fluent handwriting style with parallel ascenders.
c   Children read each word before writing it.

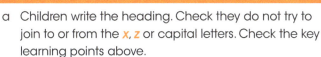
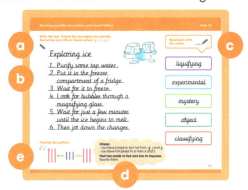

d   Self- or peer-assess: ask children to find their best two words to tick and two to improve.
e   Children finger trace and write the pattern, focusing on parallel lines.

3   Using the Workbook (p13)

Handwriting practice with a spelling focus: suffix *–tion*
a   Children trace and write the suffix.
b   Revisit the spelling rules for adding a suffix to root words ending in different ways. Children complete the activity, making verbs into nouns.
c   Challenge activity: children write the spelling rules.
d   Self- or peer-assess: ask children to check the words against the given criteria, finding two words to tick and two to improve.

4   Extra support

Small group work: Practice Book

- Children write the heading.
- Together, revisit the key learning points.
- Read the text aloud. Ask children to identify break letters.
- Children copy all or part of the text. Check the accuracy of their copying and check key learning points.

Small group work: Workbook

- Children trace and write the suffix. Ensure they check that the uprights are parallel.
- Together, read each word sum and discuss each noun. Agree the spelling.
- Work as a group to decide the spelling rules.

Homework

- PCM 12 on page 53.

5   Common errors

- Upright strokes are not parallel.
- Some letters inconsistently joined.
- Spacing irregular around break letters and incorrect joins.

Unit 13 Relative sizes of letters

Key learning

- Ascenders and descenders should be parallel and should be similar lengths; about double the x-height.
- All x-height letters are the same size.

1 Using the Interactives

Penpals gym

- Ask children to try the warm-ups: **Shoulder lift** and **Clasp and stretch**, or choose others from the reference area.

Teach

- Discuss the book titles. Explore the jokes.
- Check the key learning points. Can children identify examples of each?
- Look at the examples of children's work. Work with children to assess the texts against the key learning points.

Practise

- Children practise the pattern and use the word bank: *trader*, *settler*, *language*, *foreign*, *engravings*, *explorers*, *neighbours*, *sleigh bells*.
- The challenge word is *language*.

2 Using the Practice Book (p14)

a Children read the book titles. They write the text, focusing on a fluent handwriting style with consistently sized letters. Check the key learning points.

b Discuss the meaning of each 'read and write' word and its link to jokes. Children then write the words.

c Self- or peer-assess: ask children to find their best two words to tick and two to improve.

d Children finger trace and write the pattern, focusing on size and proportion.

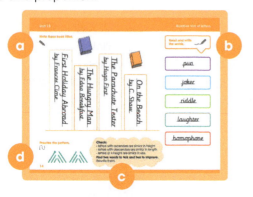

3 Using the Workbook (p14)

Handwriting practice with a spelling focus: homophones

a Children trace and copy the pairs of homophones, writing x-height letters between the lines. Check key learning points. Ask children what each word means.

b Children write a homophone for each word shown.

c Self- or peer-assess: ask children to check the words against the given criteria, finding two words to tick and two to improve.

4 Extra support

Small group work: Practice Book

- Together, revisit the key learning points.
- Read the text aloud. Talk about the jokes and identify the word play.
- Give children 5 minutes to write as much as they can.

Small group work: Workbook

- Read all of the words. Ask children to say sentences illustrating the meaning of each.
- Talk about the missing homophones. Again, ask children to say a sentence showing the meaning of each word. Next ask children to write the words.

Homework

- PCM 13 on page 54.

5 Common errors

- The angle of *g*, *f* and *j* is not consistent.
- Ascenders and descenders are too long or too short.
- x-height letters are inconsistently sized.

Unit 14 Proportion of letters

Key learning

- All lower case letters are x-height, unless they have ascenders or descenders.
- Capitals, ascenders and descenders are about double the x-height.

1 Using the Interactives

Penpals gym

- Ask children to try the warm-ups: **Bend and push** and **Finger and wrist rotate**, or choose others from the reference area.

Teach

- Discuss the text. Draw children's attention to the features identified.
- Look at the examples of children's work. Work with children to assess the texts against the key learning points.

Practise

- Children practise the pattern and use the word bank: *wait, weight, whose, who's, break, brake, allowed, aloud*.
- The challenge word is *weight*.

2 Using the Practice Book (p15)

a Talk about the two words at the top of the page. Identify good size and proportion of letters.
b Children read the poem, noting the capital letters. Discuss key learning points.
c Children write the poem using a handwriting style with good proportions.
d Discuss the meaning of each 'read and write' word. Children then write the words.

e Self- or peer-assess: ask children to find their best two words to tick and two to improve.
f Children finger trace and write the pattern, focusing on size and proportion.

3 Using the Workbook (p15)

Handwriting practice with a spelling focus: –*ture* endings
a Children trace and write the syllable. Check the key learning points.
b Children trace and write the words.
c They identify the best word to fill each gap, then they write the text.
d Self- or peer-assess: ask children to check the words against the given criteria, finding two words to tick and two to improve.

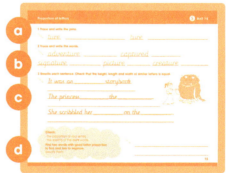

4 Extra support

Small group work: Practice Book

- Read the text aloud to children. Talk about the layout and the use of capital letters.
- Together, revisit the key learning points.
- Give children 5 minutes to write the poem.

Small group work: Workbook

- Read the syllable and discuss the sounds it represents. Children trace and write it.
- Read, trace and write the words. Check key learning points.
- Read the text aloud while children consider which word they need to fill each gap. Then they write the text.

Homework

- PCM 14 on page 54.

5 Common errors

- Letters like *e*, *w* and *s* are bigger than x-height.
- Capitals, ascenders and descenders are too large or too small and are not consistently sized.

Unit 15   Spacing between letters

Key learning

- Spacing between letters is regular.
- All upright strokes are parallel.
- Ascenders should be the same height as capital letters and descenders should be the same length.

1   Using the Interactives

Penpals gym

- Ask children to try the warm-ups: **Swimming** and **Interlocking fingers**, or choose others from the reference area.

Teach

- Introduce the text and discuss the annotations.
- Look at the examples of children's work. Work with children to assess the texts against the key learning points.

Practise

- Children practise the pattern and use the word bank: *measure, treasure, creature, temperature, furniture, nature, adventure, confusion, decision.*
- The challenge word is *nature.*

2   Using the Practice Book (p16)

a Children write the list of career opportunities. Check key learning points.

b Talk about the career each child would like to pursue. Ask them to write about their chosen career (which may not be one of those listed). Remind them to focus on the spaces between words and letters.

c Discuss the meaning of each 'read and write' word. Children then write the words.

d Self- or peer-assess: ask children to find their best two words to tick and two to improve.

e Children finger trace and write the pattern, focusing on consistent size and shape.

3   Using the Workbook (p16)

Handwriting practice with a grammar and spelling focus: *–ssion* endings

a Children trace and write the syllable. Check key learning points.

b Discuss possible noun phrases. Clarify when to choose *the*, *a* or *an*. Children write four noun phrases.

c Challenge activity: children write their own noun phrase.

d Self- or peer-assess: ask children to check the words against the given criteria, finding two words to tick and two to improve.

4   Extra support

Small group work: Practice Book

- Together, revisit the key learning points above.
- Read the text aloud to children and ask them to write down the careers.
- Talk with the children about what they would like to do. Ask each child to write two sentences about their career choice, focusing on spacing.

Small group work: Workbook

- Read the syllable and discuss the sound it represents. Then children trace and write it.
- Together, explore all of the possible alternatives for the noun phrases. Talk about which are likely to be said and which are less likely. Discuss why.
- Ask children to write their noun phrases.
- Children write their own noun phrase in pairs.

Homework

- PCM 15 on page 55.

5   Common errors

- Irregular spaces between letters due to inaccurate joining.
- x-height letters inconsistently sized.
- Uprights not parallel or not in proportion.

Unit 16   Spacing between words

Key learning

- Even spaces between words; about the length of 1–2 letter *o*s.
- Regular spaces between letters.

1   Using the Interactives

Penpals gym

- Ask children to try the warm-ups: **Arm shake** and **Clap and fist**, or choose others from the reference area.

Teach

- Read the annotations about spacing between words on the on-screen text. Consider the impact on the reader of irregular spacing or when the spaces are too wide.
- Look at the examples of children's work. Work with children to assess the texts against the key learning points.

Practise

- Children practise the pattern and use the word bank: *Dear Sir*, *Dear Mr Wilcox*, *Hi Mum*, *Yours sincerely*, *Yours faithfully*, *Lots of love*, *With best wishes*, *All the best*.
- The challenge phrase is *Hi Mum*.

2   Using the Practice Book (p17)

a Children write the heading. Check the key learning points above.

b Children read the text then write it, focusing on spacing in a fluent handwriting style.

c Children read each word before writing it.

d Self- or peer-assess: ask children to find their best two words to tick and two to improve.

e Children finger trace and write the pattern, focusing on regular spacing.

3   Using the Workbook (p17)

Handwriting practice with a spelling focus: using homophones *ai*, *ey*, *ay*, *eigh*

a Children trace and write the sentence. Check the key learning points.

b They select a spelling of the sound /ai/ to finish each word, then write the words.

c Challenge activity: children write a sentence using at least two of the words they wrote in the section above.

d Self- or peer-assess: ask children to check the words against the given criteria, finding two words to tick and two to improve.

4   Extra support

Small group work: Practice Book

- Ask children to write the heading. Together, revisit the key learning points above.
- Read the text aloud to children.
- Children identify and practice any joins they think will be tricky for them.
- Next they copy the text for 5 minutes.
- Check the accuracy of their copying and the key learning points.

Small group work: Workbook

- Ask children to trace and write the sentence. Check key learning points.
- Together, identify the words that can be made by adding /ai/ and model strategies for selecting the appropriate spelling before children complete the task.
- Children should compose a shared sentence orally before writing it.

Homework

- PCM 16 on page 55.

5   Common errors

- Spaces between words are uneven or are too wide or too cramped.
- Inaccurate joins mean spaces between letters are uneven.

Unit 17 Writing at speed

Key learning

- Clear, legible writing at speed with good spacing and parallel uprights.
- All letters should be joined except break letters *g, y, j, x, z*.

1 Using the Interactives

Penpals gym

- Ask children to try the warm-ups: **Neck stretch** and **Finger point**, or choose others from the reference area.

Teach

- Discuss the on-screen text. Agree that all words are synonyms of *quickly*. Ask children what happens to their handwriting when they write at speed.
- Look at the examples of children's work. Work with children to assess the texts against the key learning points.

Practise

- Children practise the pattern and use the word bank: *hissed, whispered, sighed, moaned, said, exclaimed, cried, bawled, bellowed*.
- The challenge word is *hissed*.

2 Using the Practice Book (p18)

a   Children will need access to a stopwatch, either individually or on-screen. They read the words and recognise that they are all synonyms. Check key learning points.

b   Children write the 20 words (four repeats of five words), timing themselves with a stopwatch. Prompt them to annotate their writing as stated. Ask children to write one iteration of each word at normal speed to compare.

c   Read and write: discuss the meaning of each synonym. Children then write the words carefully.

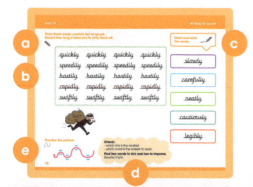

d   Self- or peer-assess: ask children to find their best two words to tick and two to improve.

e   Children finger trace and write the pattern, focusing on spacing.

3 Using the Workbook (p18)

Handwriting practice with a punctuation focus: inverted commas ("speech marks")

a   Children trace the words carefully then write them quickly. Check key learning points.

b   Discuss the best synonym to fill the gaps. Children write in the missing words at speed.

c   Challenge activity: children add punctuation and show the punctuation they used.

d   Self- or peer-assess: ask children to check the words against the given criteria, finding two words to tick and two to improve.

4 Extra support

Small group work: Practice Book

- Discuss the key learning points.
- Read the words aloud to children. Identify the synonyms.
- Children write each word once, neatly.
- They then time themselves writing the 20 words.
- Talk with the children about the impact of speed on their handwriting. Let them individually explain what they observe.

Small group work: Workbook

- Read and talk about the synonyms. Children trace, then write at speed.
- Together, agree the best word to fill each gap.
- Children first fill in the missing words at speed.
- Together, agree punctuation.

Homework

- PCM 17 on page 56.

5 Common errors

- Handwriting is not legible at speed.
- Formation of some letters or joins is not accurate.
- Upright strokes are not parallel.
- Size of letters is not regular or not in proportion.

Unit 18   Improving fluency

Key learning

- Clear, legible writing at speed.
- All letters should be joined except break letters *g, y, j, x, z.*
- Consider letter formation, parallel uprights, size and spacing.

1   Using the Interactives

Penpals gym

- Ask children to try the warm-ups: **Scissors** and **Knuckles, wrists and palms**, or choose others from the reference area.

Teach

- Discuss the text, identifying its purpose. Children identify key features that lead to legibility.
- Look at the examples of children's work. Work with children to assess the texts against the key learning points.

Practise

- Children practise the pattern and use the word bank: *I'm, He's, You're, They're, We're, He'd, You'd, They'd, We'd.*
- The challenge word is *I'm.*

2   Using the Practice Book (p19)

a   Children work out the order of each segment in the letter. Check key learning points.

b   Children write the letter using a fast, fluent and legible handwriting style. They should time themselves with a stopwatch and record how long it takes them. Ask children to compare this handwriting with the very fast writing from the last session. What are the key differences?

c   Discuss when each sign-off would be most appropriate. Then ask children to write the words.

d   Self- or peer-assess: ask children to find their best two words to tick and two to improve.

e   Children finger trace and write the pattern, focusing on control.

3   Using the Workbook (p19)

Handwriting practice with a grammar focus: standard English *was/were*

a   Children trace and write the words using a fast and fluent handwriting style. Check key learning points

b   They read the sentences and correct the errors. They write the sentences in a fast and fluent style.

c   Self- or peer-assess: ask children to check the words against the given criteria, finding two words to tick and two to improve.

4   Extra support

Small group work: Practice Book

- Together, revisit the key learning points above.
- Read the text aloud and agree the order of the letter.
- Give children 5 minutes to write as much of the letter as they can. Remind them of expectations.
- Talk about when they should use fast and fluent handwriting and when speed is necessary.

Small group work: Workbook

- Talk about the importance of subject/verb agreement.
- Together, identify and correct the errors.
- Ask children to write the sentences correctly using a fast, fluent and legible handwriting style.

Homework

- PCM 18 on page 56.

5   Common errors

- Handwriting is rigid, not fluent.
- At speed, accuracy of letter formation at joins is inconsistent.
- Writing is not well spaced and uprights are not parallel.

Key learning

- Clear, legible writing at speed.
- All letters should be joined except break letters *g, y, j, x, z*.
- Consider parallel uprights, size and spacing.

1   Using the Interactives

Penpals gym

- Ask children to try the warm-ups: **Press down** and **Parallel lines**, or choose others from the reference area.

Teach

- Discuss the text. Identify handwriting features that are vulnerable when writing at speed.
- Look at the examples of children's work. Work with children to assess the texts against the key learning points.

Practise

- Children practise the pattern and use the word bank: *I, mine, you, yours, she, hers, he, his, it, its, we, ours, they, theirs*.
- The challenge words are *I, mine*.

2   Using the Practice Book (p20)

a   Discuss key learning points. Give children 5 minutes to write the recount at speed, using a fast, fluent and legible handwriting style. Note how much they manage to complete in 5 minutes. Ask children to compare this handwriting with what they did in the past two sessions. What are they key differences? What changes at speed? Check their friends can read their handwriting.

b   Children read and write the words – first carefully, then fast and fluent, and finally as fast as possible. Identify key differences.

c   Self- or peer-assess: ask children to find their best two words to tick and two to improve.

d   Children finger trace and write the pattern neatly, then speedily.

3   Using the Workbook (p20)

Handwriting practice with a grammar focus: possessive pronouns

a   Children trace and write the pronouns using a fast and fluent handwriting style. Together, identify which is the personal pronoun and which is the possessive. Check key learning points.

b   Children read the sentences and decide which pronoun is missing. Ask them to write the corrected sentences using a fast and fluent style.

c   Challenge activity: children write a sentence using a different pronoun.

d   Self- or peer-assess: ask children to check their writing against the given criteria, finding two words to tick and two to improve.

4   Extra support

Small group work: Practice Book

- Together, revisit the key learning points above.
- Read the text aloud to children.
- Give children 5 minutes to write as much of the text as they can. Remind them of expectations.
- Talk about when they should use fast and fluent handwriting and when speed is necessary.

Small group work: Workbook

- Talk about when pronouns are used.
- Together, identify and write the correct pronouns.
- Ask children to write the sentences correctly using a fast, fluent and legible handwriting style.

Homework

- PCM 19 on page 57.

5   Common errors

- Spacing is irregular and uprights are not parallel.
- Letters like *a* and *g* are not closed at the top and those like *u* and *y* are not open.

Key learning

- Focus on consistent relative size of all letters.
- Take care with spacing between letters.
- Parallel ascenders and descenders.
- All letters are joined except break letters *g, y, j, x, z*.

1 Using the Practice Book (p21)

a Read the assessment text. Tell children they can choose to use some of the 'read and write' words when they fill in the gaps. Check the key learning points above.

b Children write the text, self-assessing as they go and filling in the gaps. Encourage children to write their own targets for improvement.

c Children read each word before writing it first slowly and then at speed.

d Children finger trace and write the pattern.

2 Using the Workbook (p21)

a Check key learning points (and common errors). Remind children to look back through the Workbook if they are unclear of the answers to any of the questions. Get children to trace all tinted writing and to answer the questions, writing quickly and fluently.

b Self- or peer-assess: ask children to mark their own or each other's work.

3 Extra support

Small group work: Practice Book

- Together, revisit the key learning points.
- Read the text aloud. Ask each child to decide how to finish each sentence. Encourage them to look back at recent work, both in handwriting and in curriculum books, to inform their decision.
- Children write the assessment.
- Check the accuracy of their copying and discuss their self-assessments.
- Agree personal targets and reviews those from last term.

Small group work: Workbook

- Look at each question together, working out answers and offering practice opportunities.
- Let children work independently. Check accuracy of spelling and punctuation.
- Children should mark their own or each other's work, with support.

Homework

- PCM 20 on page 57.

Unit 21   Consistency of size

Key learning

- Lower case letters the same size as *x*.

1   Using the Interactives

Penpals gym

- Ask children to try the warm-ups: **Hand shake** and **Bounce fingertips**, or choose others from the reference area.

Teach

- Discuss the text and its annotations. Talk about why it is important that letters are a consistent size.
- Look at the examples of children's work. Work with children to assess the texts against the key learning points.

Practise

- Children practise the pattern and use the word bank: *young*, *double*, *country*, *touch*, *trouble*, *encourage*, *nourish*, *countryside*.
- The challenge word is *countryside*.

2   Using the Practice Book (p22)

a   Children write the heading, noting where capitals are used. Check the key learning points.

b   They read and write the text, focusing on a fluent handwriting style with consistently sized letters.

c   Self- or peer-assess: ask children to find their best two words to tick and two to improve.

d   Children finger trace and write the pattern, focusing on regular size.

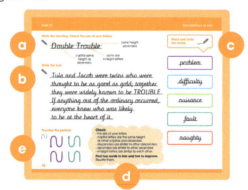

3   Using the Workbook (p22)

Handwriting practice with a spelling focus: pronouncing *ou*

a   Children trace and write the joins and phrase using a fast and fluent handwriting style and focusing on the size of the letters. Check key learning points.

b   Children read, trace and write the words, considering how *ou* is pronounced in each. Then they write the words in the correct set, writing between the lines drawn.

c   Challenge activity: children add one more word to each set.

d   Self- or peer-assess: ask children to check the words against the given criteria, finding two words to tick and two to improve.

4   Extra support

Small group work: Practice Book

- Read the text aloud to children.
- Children identify where and why capital letters are used. Check key learning points.
- Support children as they copy the text.
- Check the accuracy of their copying and the size of their letters.

Small group work: Workbook

- Talk about different ways of pronouncing *ou*.
- Ask children to read, trace and then write the phrase.
- Together, discuss and agree to which set each word belongs and suggest further words to include.
- Children then write the words.

Homework

- PCM 21 on page 58.

5   Common errors

- Letters like *e*, *w* and *s* are not x-height.
- Capitals, ascenders and descenders are more or less than twice as long as x-height letters.

Unit 22   Proportion

Key learning

- Lower case letters the same size as *x*.
- Capitals, ascenders and descenders are twice as long as x-height letters.

1   Using the Interactives

Penpals gym

- Ask children to try the warm-ups: **Hands push down** and **Rotating wrists**, or choose others from the reference area.

Teach

- Discuss the text and its annotations. Talk about why it is important that handwriting is consistently sized.
- Look at the examples of children's work. Work with children to assess the texts against the key learning points.

Practise

- Children practise the pattern and use the word bank: *Egypt, pyjamas, myth, bicycle, pyramid, mystery, rhyme, rhythm*.
- The challenge word is *pyramid*.

2   Using the Practice Book (p23)

a   Children write the heading. Check key learning points.
b   Then read the book titles, noting where capitals are used. Then, they write the text. Remind them to focus on a fluent handwriting style with consistently sized letters and appropriate proportions.
c   Children read each word before writing it.
d   Self- or peer-assess: ask children to find their best two words to tick and two to improve.
e   Children finger trace and write the pattern, focusing on proportion.

3   Using the Workbook (p23)

Handwriting practice with a spelling focus: pronouncing *y*
a   Children trace and write the phrase. Check key learning points.
b   Children read, trace and write the words, deciding how *y* is pronounced in each. They write the words in the correct set.
c   Self- or peer-assess: ask children to check the words against the given criteria, finding two words to tick and two to improve.

4   Extra support

Small group work: Practice Book

- Children write the heading. Check key learning points.
- Read the book titles aloud.
- Children identify where and why capital letters are used and copy some or all of the titles.
- Check the accuracy of their copying and their handwriting.

Small group work: Workbook

- Talk about different ways of pronouncing *y*.
- Children read, trace and then write the phrase.
- Discuss and agree to which set each word belongs and suggest further words to include.
- Children trace and then write the words in the correct set.

Homework

- PCM 22 on page 58.

5   Common errors

- Capitals, ascenders and descenders are much more or less than twice the length of x-height letters.
- Ascenders and descenders vary in length.

Unit 23 Spacing between letters and words

Key learning

- Spaces between letters and words should be even.

1 Using the Interactives

Penpals gym

- Ask children to try the warm-ups: **Shoulder moves** and **Clap and fist**, or choose others from the reference area.

Teach

- Discuss the annotations on the on-screen text.
- Look at the examples of children's work. Work with children to assess the texts against the key learning points.

Practise

- Children practise the pattern and use the word bank: *serious face, enormous slug, dangerous tiger, poisonous, snake, various people, venomous snake, tremendous enthusiasm, jealous toddler, courageous friend.*
- The challenge phrase is *poisonous snake*.

2 Using the Practice Book (p24)

a Children write the heading, focusing on advice in the annotations.

b They read the definitions and then write them. Explain that they should focus on a fluent handwriting style with consistent spaces between the letters and words.

c Children read each word before writing it to practise managing consistency of spacing.

d Self- or peer-assess: ask children to find their best two words to tick and two to improve.

e Children finger trace and write the pattern, focusing on regular spacing.

3 Using the Workbook (p24)

Handwriting practice with a spelling focus: noun phrases

a Children trace and write the joins and the phrase. Check key learning points.

b They trace and write the phrase.

c Children must decide how to combine the different words and phrases to create expanded noun phrases. Then they write their chosen phrases.

d Self- or peer-assess: ask children to check the words against the given criteria, finding two words to tick and two to improve.

4 Extra support

Small group work: Practice Book

- Children write the heading, then revisit the key learning points.
- Read the definitions aloud to children. Discuss where they would expect to find definitions.
- Children write the definitions.
- Check the accuracy of their copying and their handwriting.

Small group work: Workbook

- Children read, trace and write the joins and phrase.
- Talk about different ways of expanding a noun phrase.
- Together, discuss how the different elements can be combined. Model writing some.
- Ask children to write their expanded noun phrases.

Homework

- PCM 23 on page 59.

5 Common errors

- Inaccurate joins from letters such as *r, f, s, b, p* leads to inaccurate spacing of letters.
- Words are more or less than 1–2 letter *o*s apart.

Key learning

- All lower case letters should be x-height unless they have ascenders or descenders.
- Ascenders and descenders are twice x-height.
- Spacing between letters and words is regular and appropriate.

1   Using the Interactives

Penpals gym

- Ask children to try the warm-ups: **Stretch** and **Clap and grasp**, or choose others from the reference area.

Teach

- Discuss the annotations shown on the screen.
- Look at the examples of children's work. Work with children to assess the texts against the key learning points.

Practise

- Children practise the pattern and use the word bank: *Before*, *The next morning*, *After lunch*, *Earlier*, *Rarely*, *Afterwards*, *Sometimes*, *Occasionally*.
- The challenge adverbial is *After lunch*.

2   Using the Practice Book (p25)

a Children write the heading. Refer to the key learning objectives and annotations.

b They use a ruler to draw a table, then read the adverbials and decide which category they fit into. They write the adverbials (with initial capital letter) into the table.

c Children read each word before writing it.

d Self- or peer-assess: ask children to find their best two words to tick and two to improve.

e Children finger trace and write the pattern, focusing on consistent size and spacing.

3   Using the Workbook (p25)

Handwriting practice with a grammar focus: fronted adverbials

a Children trace and write the sentence. Check key learning points.

b Children read and then say the sentence with fronted adverbials, aloud. Then they write their new sentences.

c Self- or peer-assess: ask children to check the words against the given criteria, finding two words to tick and two to improve.

4   Extra support

Small group work: Practice Book

- Chilren write the heading. Check the key learning points.
- Discuss the adverbials, linking this to previous learning.
- Provide a copy of the table for children to use. Together, agree how to complete it. Children finish the task independently.

Small group work: Workbook

- Remind children how to front adverbials and talk about the impact of doing so.
- Then children read, trace and write the first sentence.
- Together, agree what each revised sentence will be before the children tackle writing the new sentences.

Homework

- PCM 24 on page 59.

5   Common errors

- Height of lower case letters is inconsistent.
- Some ascenders and descenders are out of proportion.
- Spacing between letters and words is inconsistent.

Unit 25   Fluency: writing longer words

Key learning

- Appropriate pen breaks are taken in long words.
- Joins and spacing are consistent.

1 Using the Interactives

Penpals gym

- Ask children to try the warm-ups: **Curved back** and **Finger and wrist rotate**, or choose others from the reference area.

Teach

- Discuss the text and evaluate using key learning points. Agree where pen breaks could be taken.
- Look at the examples of children's work. Work with children to assess the texts against the key learning points.

Practise

- Children practise the pattern and use the word bank: *misunderstanding, misbehave, misspell, mislead, disappointment, disagree, disobey, disappear.*
- The challenge phrase is *disobey.*

2 Using the Practice Book (p26)

a Ask children to write the heading. Check the key learning points above.

b Discuss purpose and layout of the advert. Ask children to copy the advert using a fast and fluent style with good joins and consistent size, proportion and spacing. Ask them to consider whether they need pen breaks during the longer words.

c Children read each word before writing it.

d Self- or peer-assess: ask children to find their best two words to tick and two to improve.

e Children finger trace and write the pattern, focusing on consistent spacing.

3 Using the Workbook (p26)

Handwriting practice with a grammar focus: standard English *have done*/*has done*

a Children trace and write the phrases using a fast and fluent handwriting style. Check key learning points.

b Children read the sentences and identify the errors. Then they write the sentences, correcting the errors.

c Self- or peer-assess: ask children to check the words against the given criteria, finding two words to tick and two to improve.

4 Extra support

Small group work: Practice Book

- Children write the heading. Revisit the key learning points.
- Can children identify the purpose of the text? How do they know? Read the advert aloud.
- Identify where pen breaks might be taken in the longer words. Children write the text.
- Check the accuracy of their copying.

Small group work: Workbook

- Focus on the opening phrases. Ask children to say sentences using each one. Talk about the differences between the phrases.
- Together, identify and correct the errors.
- Children write the corrected sentences at speed.

Homework

- PCM 25 on page 60.

5 Common errors

- Pen breaks are not taken or inappropriately placed.
- Pen breaks lead to inappropriate spacing within words.

Unit 26 Speed and fluency

Key learning

- Even, legible, joined handwriting is fluent and fast.
- All letters should be joined except break letters *g, y, j, x, z*.

1 Using the Interactives

Penpals gym

- Ask children to try the warm-ups: **Swimming** and **Fist and stretch**, or choose others from the reference area.

Teach

- Discuss the text, evaluating it against each of the key learning points.
- Look at the examples of children's work. Work with children to assess the texts against the key learning points.

Practise

- Children practise the pattern and use the word bank: *me, mine, you, yours, him, his, her, hers, us, ours, them, theirs, it, its*.
- The challenge words are *us, ours*.

2 Using the Practice Book (p27)

a Children write the heading. Check key learning points above.

b Read the text together. Start the timer while children write the text, fast and fluently. Ask them to count how many words they have written. Reset the time and ask the children to repeat the activity.

c Children read each word before writing it.

d Self- or peer-assess: ask children to find their best two words to tick and two to improve.

e Children finger trace and write the pattern, focusing on regularity of form.

3 Using the Workbook (p27)

Handwriting practice with a spelling focus: prefixes *–dis, –mis*

a Children trace and write the prefix. Check key learning points.

b Ask them to write the words, twice each, without taking pen breaks. Prompt them to identify their most fluent word.

c Children decide which prefix will be needed for each word, then they write the words quickly and fluently.

d Challenge activity: children write the spelling rule for adding *mis*– to *spell*.

e Self- or peer-assess: ask children to check the words against the given criteria, finding two words to tick and two to improve.

4 Extra support

Small group work: Practice Book

- Children write the heading. Check key learning points.
- Read the text aloud in sections. Ask children to write just the section of text you read aloud each time. Before reading each section, tell children whether you want them write normally, or quickly and fluently.

Small group work: Workbook

- Discuss the prefixes. What do children remember about them and their meaning?
- Once they have written each of the words twice, check against key learning points.
- Together, discuss the words they can create by adding prefixes. They write these words.

Homework

- PCM 26 on page 60.

5 Common errors

- Inconsistent or inaccurate joins lead to irregular spacing.

Unit 27   Revising break letters

Key learning

- All letters should be joined except break letters *g, y, j, x, z*.
- Spacing around break letters should be consistent with other spacing within a word.

1   Using the Interactives

Penpals gym

- Ask children to try the warm-ups: **Arms high** and **Hand clap**, or choose others from the reference area.

Teach

- Discuss why each letter is a break letter, i.e. *g, j, y* all end with a movement to the left, *x* finishes to the left and *z* is composed entirely of straight lines.
- Look at the examples of children's work. Work with children to assess the texts against the key learning points.

Practise

- Children practise the pattern and use the word bank: *triangular, mixture, jigsaw puzzle, always, naughty, injured, anxiously, amazing*.
- The challenge word is *naughty*.

2   Using the Practice Book (p28)

a   Children write the break letters. Check key learning points.

b   Read the words aloud and try to work out what each one means. Challenge children to identify the non-words and to check in a dictionary. Children write the words, using break letters for pen breaks. Ask them to ring the non-words.

c   Children read each word before writing it.

d   Self- or peer-assess: ask children to find their best two words to tick and two to improve.

e   Children finger trace and write the pattern, focusing on regularity of form.

3   Using the Workbook (p28)

Handwriting practice with a grammar focus: pronouns

a   Children write the sets of pronouns. Check key learning points.

b   Focus children's attention on the pronoun outside each speech bubble and tell them that the pronouns outside and within the speech bubble must match. Ask them to say what will be in the bubble before they write the missing pronouns.

c   Self- or peer-assess: ask children to check the words against the given criteria, finding two words to tick and two to improve.

4   Extra support

Small group work: Practice Book

- Children write the break letters. Check key learning points.
- Read the words aloud. Challenge children to identify the non-words. Together, check in a maths dictionary and find the meanings of the real words.
- Children write the words, using break letters for pen breaks.

Small group work: Workbook

- Discuss the pronouns. What do children remember about them and when they are used?
- Together, discuss how the speech bubbles will be worded. Then children complete them.

Homework

- PCM 27 on page 61.

5   Common errors

- Spacing around break letters is irregular.
- Inaccurate joining means spacing between other letters is irregular.

Unit 28   Print alphabet: presentation

Key learning

- Print is used for clarity in notices and labelling.
- No joining or exit flicks from letters.
- Same expectations about size, proportion and spacing as for most handwriting.
- Letter formation and clarity of writing.

1   Using the Interactives

Penpals gym

- Ask children to try the warm-ups: **Shoulder lift** and **Interlocking rings**, or choose others from the reference area.

Teach

- Discuss the text and agree that it is most likely that a notice like this will be written in print letters. Discuss why.
- Look at the examples of children's work. Work with children to assess the texts against the key learning points.

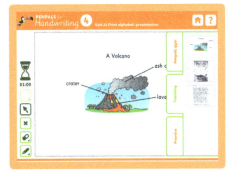

Practise

- Children practise the pattern and use the word bank:
  a b c, d e f, g h i, j k l, m n o, p q r, s t u, v w y z.

2   Using the Practice Book (p29)

a   Ask children to print the heading. Check the key learning points above.

b   Read and discuss the text. Draw children's attention to the text's function. Remind them to focus on print alphabet with consistent size, proportion and spacing.

c   Children read each word before writing it in print.

d   Self- or peer-assess: ask children to find their best two words to tick and two to improve.

e   Children finger trace and write the pattern.

3   Using the Workbook (p29)

Handwriting practice: presentation: print alphabet

a   Ask children to complete the alphabet.

b   Children write the whole print alphabet. Check the key learning points.

c   Children print their name and address.

d   Challenge activity: children write a brief explanation of when and why we use print.

e   Self- or peer-assess: ask children to check the letters against the key learning point.

4   Extra support

Small group work: Practice Book

- Provide print alphabet strips to copy if necessary.
- Read the text. Talk about its function. Discuss why it is in print rather than in script. Check key learning points.
- Children write the heading and the text.

Small group work: Workbook

- Can children recite the alphabet?
- Can they complete it without copying? If not, provide an alphabet strip.
- Check formation of print letters as children write the print alphabet and then their names and addresses.
- Children should identify two letters to tick and two to improve.

Homework

- PCM 28 on page 61.

5   Common errors

- Adding exit flicks or joining.
- Irregular letter sizing.

Unit 29 Assessment

Key learning

- Even, legible, joined handwriting is fluent and fast.
- All letters should be joined except break letters *g, y, j, x, z.*

1 Using the Practice Book (pp30–31)

a Ask children to read the text. Explain that the list on p31 gives the criteria for success.

b Talk about the layout and the use of print for the headings. Revisit key learning points.

c Self- or peer-assess: ask children to read each statement on page 31. They should write the statement number and add a ✓ or a ✗ to show whether they think they have achieved it.

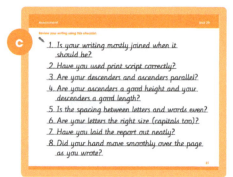

2 Using the Workbook (p30)

a Explain that the assessment uses words and spelling patterns from throughout the year. Children should trace and complete each word and then write the whole word. They will need to use some of the letter strings in the cloud at the foot of the page.

b Self- or peer assess: when they have finished, children should check their spelling and consider their handwriting, finding two words to tick and two to improve.

3 Extra support

Small group work: Practice Book

- Read the text together. Ask children to tell you what its purpose is. Check key learning points
- Discuss the layout, heading and subheadings as well as the main text.
- Give children 5 minutes to write as much of the text as they can.
- Then read through the list of assessment criteria on page 31 and ask children to self-assess against them, one statement at a time.

Small group work: Workbook

- Together, talk through the words one at a time.
- Ask children to tell you what they think each word might be, based on the letters they can see. Accept any suggestion that meets the criteria.
- If children do not know, look through the Workbook together to identify possibilities.

Homework

- PCM 29 on page 62.

Unit 30 Capital letters: presentation

Key learning

- Letter formation.
- No joining to or from any capital.
- Consistency of size; parallel upright strokes.

1 Using the Interactives

Penpals gym

- Ask children to try the warm-ups: **Backwards bends** and **Clap and fist**, or choose others from the reference area.

Teach

- Discuss the text. Do children recognise this? Talk about the consistency of size and spacing in each line.
- Look at the examples of children's work. Work with children to assess the poster against the key learning points.

Practise

- Children practise the pattern and use the word bank:
  A B C, D E F, G H I, J K L, M N O, P Q R, S T U, V W X Y.

2 Using the Practice Book (p31)

a Where might children have seen a sign like this before? Focus on layout: each line must be the same size and evenly spaced.

b Children read each line before writing it.

c Self- or peer-assess: ask children to find their best two rows to tick and two to improve.

d Children finger trace and write the pattern, focusing on size and spacing.

3 Using the Workbook (p31)

Handwriting practice: presentation: capital letters

a Ask children to complete the capitals alphabet. Check key learning points.

b Children should write the words in clear, consistently sized capitals.

c Self- or peer-assess: ask children to check their work against the given criteria, finding two words to tick and two to improve.

4 Extra support

Small group work: Practice Book

- Before children write the text, ask them to write the alphabet in capital letters. Provide alphabet strips to copy if necessary.
- Read the text. Talk about its function.
- Provide line guides showing top and bottom of letters for each line. Ask children to write the text.

Small group work: Workbook

- If children do not know the alphabet, provide an alphabet strip.
- Model the words in capitals before children write them.

Homework

- PCM 30 on page 62.

5 Common errors

- Inaccurate letter shape.
- Uprights not parallel.
- Size and spacing irregular.

Name .... Date ....

Write words that have *bl* or *ph* in them.

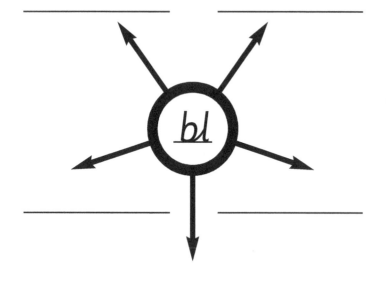

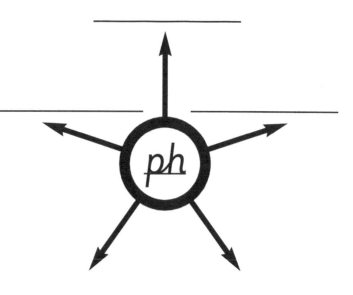

Name .... Date ....

Write the joins.   Match and write the words from the box below.

bi	*bi*	*bin*
bu		
pi		
pu		

bin	*puppy*	*pizza*	*bump*
pull	*bicycle*	*button*	*picnic*

Name ....   Date ....

Write the joins.   Match and write the words from the box below.

ba   *ba* _____   *bank* _____

bo _____

pa _____

po _____

| *bank* | *polish* | *pattern* | *bounce* |
| *power* | *parrot* | *bottle* | *bandit* |

Name ....   Date ....

Trace and write the joins.

pp _____   *bb* _____

Rewrite these words in alphabetical order.

	Practise here	Fast and fluent
opposite	_____	_____
suppose	_____	_____
robber	_____	_____
gobble	_____	_____
wrapper	_____	_____
appear	_____	_____
abbreviate	_____	_____

Name ....   Date ....

Trace and write the letters.

X _____   Z _____

Match the definitions to the words.

like a striped horse _____   _____

you put things in these _____   _____

a type of deer _____   _____

something you do in science _____   _____

very bad snow storm _____   _____

when a boat turns over _____   _____

zebra   gazelle   boxes   capsize   experiment   blizzard

Name ....   Date ....

Rewrite the words.

	Practise here	Fast and fluent
accidentally	_____	_____
business	_____	_____
caught	_____	_____
different	_____	_____
eighth	_____	_____
favourite	_____	_____
guard	_____	_____

Unit 7 Consistent size of letters

7

Name .... Date ....

Sort the words. Think about the size of your letters within a word and between words.

disobey *inaccurate* *mislead* *disrespect*
disappoint *misbehave* *inactive*
misspell *incorrect* *misplace* *disagree*

Prefix dis-	Prefix mis-	Prefix in-

Unit 8 Relative size of capitals

8

Name .... Date ....

Write the alphabet in capitals.

Rewrite the information in capitals.

Sometimes we use capital
letters to suggest that we
(or a character) is shouting
or to give emphasis. Really?
Yes.

How even are the sizes of your capital letters?

Name .... Date ....

Rewrite these phrases.

	Very fast	Very neatly
six characters		
the antique		
weigh the medal		
action stations		
in it to win it		

Name .... Date ....

Check the spacing of letters and punctuation. Write the speech.

"Where's my Hair-r-ry To-o-oe?
Who's got my Hair-r-ry To-o-oe?
YOU'VE got it!"

_____

_____

_____

Why is spacing important?

Name ....   Date ....

Write the phrases. Check the ascenders are parallel.

	First try	Second try
parallel lines	_____	_____
tall letters	_____	_____
downstrokes	_____	_____
side by side	_____	_____
adjacent lines	_____	_____
lots of lines	_____	_____

Name ....   Date ....

Write a word for each of the break letters *g, j, x, y, z* that also includes ascenders.

Word		Try 1	Try 2
g	*allergy*	*allergy*	_____
j	_____	_____	_____
x	_____	_____	_____
y	_____	_____	_____
z	_____	_____	_____

Why are parallel ascenders important?

Name ....   Date ....

Write each set of letters twice. Check the size of your letters.

aeiou   *tkth*

_____   _____   _____   _____

abcde   *owow*

_____   _____   _____   _____

sfsf   *klmnopq*

_____   _____   _____   _____

Name ....   Date ....

Trace and write the join.   *ious* _____

Match the nouns and adjectives.

suspicion   _____

infection   _____

conscience   _____

glory   _____

labour   _____

seriousness   _____

infectious

glorious

laborious

conscious

suspicious

serious

Name _____   Date _____

Contract the words using an apostrophe. Check the spacing in each word.

they have   _____   *were not*   _____

you will   _____   *should not*   _____

he is   _____   *would not*   _____

she would   _____   *have not*   _____

could not   _____   *what will*   _____

did not   _____   *let us*   _____

Name _____   Date _____

Write out the words in full. Check the spacing between each word. Watch out for punctuation spaces, too.

Later that day, Rex's best friend, Dan, rang.

_____

"Look out!" he cried. "It's about to fall."

_____

I'll pack a T-shirt, shorts and a sweatshirt.

_____

Name _____ Date _____

Write the pangrams (sentences that contain the entire alphabet).

The quick brown fox jumps over the lazy dog.

_____

_____

The public was amazed to view the quickness
and dexterity of the juggler.

_____

_____

Name _____ Date _____

Sort the words into phrases.

home the team _____ .

big boys some _____ .

clown an on elephant _____ .

girl's every dream _____ .

players there over those _____ .

parents your, my parents _____ .

good team a _____ .

Name ....   Date ....

Write each word in a phrase or sentence.

seen/scene   *way/weigh*   *peace/piece*

_____   _____

_____   _____

_____   _____

_____   _____

Although fast, is your handwriting legible?

Name ....   Date ....

Write the limerick at speed in joined writing.

There was a young farmer   _____

from Leeds   _____

Who swallowed two   _____

packets of seeds.   _____

It soon came to pass,   _____

He was covered in grass,   _____

And he couldn't sit down   _____

for the weeds.   _____

Name ....   Date ....

Ring what's wrong. Rewrite correctly.

	First try	Second try
Double Trouble		
double time		
double space		
triple check		
triple jump		
triple play		

Name ....   Date ....

Write these funny book titles. Check your letter proportions.

The Arctic Ocean by I.C. Waters

Whodunnit? by Ivor Clew

Winning the Lottery by Jack Pott

Catching Criminals by Hans Upp

(23)

Name ....   Date ....

Write each prefix or suffix. Check the spacing of the letters. Then write a word for each.

–ation

anti–

auto–

_____   _____   _____

_____   _____   _____

super–

inter–

–ly

_____   _____   _____

_____   _____   _____

---

(24)

Name ....   Date ....

Fill the gaps with the adverbials.

meanwhile   earlier   afterwards   then

now   some months later

She left much _____ *than me.*

She was sorry _____ *but* _____

realised it was too late. _____ *I'd told*

everyone about it. _____ *we were*

friends again and _____ *we see each other a lot.*

Check size, proportion and spacing to make sure your writing is legible.

Name .... Date ....

Write the invitation in smooth, fluent writing.

Dear Joe

Please come to my party on Saturday 28th August at 7.30pm at Saint Benedict's Hall. There'll be a magician! Please let me know a.s.a.p.

Will.

_____

_____

_____

_____

_____

_____

Name .... Date ....

Use each dialogue word once.
Write fast and fluently.

*asked agreed crowed blurted
shouted replied whispered*

"I won," _____ Tom.

"You did," _____ Sam, "but don't show off."

"I'm the best," _____ Tom.

"Well done," _____ Sam. He sniffed. "It's not fair though," he _____ out. "You started first."

"Are you saying that I cheated?" _____ Tom.

"Yes," _____ Sam.

Name .... Date ....

Write the hobby words in alphabetical order. Label each picture.

Write the words in alphabetical order.

_____

_____

_____

_____

_____

_____

Name .... Date ....

Sort these things into lists. Print them.

Sweet food	Savoury food	Drink
_____	_____	_____
_____	_____	_____
_____	_____	_____

chocolate	cheese	jam
peanuts	water	milk
cola	cake	crisps

Name ....   Date ....

Choose a piece of your own handwriting.

Read the statements and fill in the table.

Practise any joins you need to improve.

	Yes	No
1 The letters are all formed correctly.		
2 The letters all rest on the line except for the descenders, which hang below it.		
3 The small letters are all the same size.		
4 Ascenders and descenders are the same length and are parallel.		
5 Capital letters are not joined. They are the same height as ascenders.		
6 Diagonal joins are all made correctly.		
7 Horizontal joins are all made correctly.		
8 The slope of the writing is even.		
9 The writing was done quickly and smoothly.		
10 The writing is clear, easy to read, and well presented, with print letters used for headings, labels and captions.		

Unit 30   Capital letters: presentation   30

Name ....   Date ....

Try out different ways to write capital letters.

HEY!

WOW!

LOL!

Try your own:

a b c d e f g h i j k l m n o p q r s t u v w x y z

Penpals
writing mat
for right-handers

A B C D E F G H I J K L M N O P Q R S T U V W X Y Z

---

a b c d e f g h i j k l m n o p q r s t u v w x y z

Penpals
writing mat
for left-handers

A B C D E F G H I J K L M N O P Q R S T U V W X Y Z

Variations in font throughout *Penpals*

FIVE DEVELOPMENTAL PHASES	FONT USED	*Penpals* Progression	*Penpals* typesizes
1 GROSS AND FINE MOTOR SKILLS, PATTERN-MAKING AND LETTER FORMATION	*a b c d*	Each letter family is introduced with finger tracing letters incorporating the letter family artwork and a starting dot. Hollow letters with starting dots and arrows to show correct letter formation are also used for finger tracing. Solid letters with starting dots support letter formation. Independent writing with exit flicks is encouraged in preparation for joining.	*a a* **Foundation 2/Primary 1** 21mm/11mm *a a* **Year 1/Primary 2** 8mm/5mm *a a* **Year 2/Primary 3** 7mm/4mm
2 SECURING CORRECT LETTER FORMATION	*pen*	Joins are introduced from year 1.	*a a* **Year 3/Primary 4** 5mm/4mm
3 SECURING THE JOINS	*secure*	Once all joins have been taught, all words are shown as joined for practice and consolidation (with the exception of the break letters).	*a a* **Year 4/Primary 5** 5mm/4mm
4 SECURING THE JOINS; LEGIBILITY, CONSISTENCY, QUALITY	*faster*	Children are encouraged to develop an individual style for speed and legibility.	*a* **Year 5/Primary 6** 4mm
5 SPEED, FLUENCY AND PERSONAL STYLE	*individual* *print* *jokey*	Further development of an individual style as well as presentation skills and techniques. At this stage break letters may be joined.	*a a* **Year 6/Primary 7** 4mm/3mm